Phonics and Spelling

Ages 9–10

Julie Crimmins-Crocker

Published by Collins
An imprint of HarperCollins*Publishers*
77–85 Fulham Palace Road
Hammersmith
London
W6 8JB

**Browse the complete Collins catalogue at
www.collinseducation.com**

© HarperCollins*Publishers* Limited 2011, on behalf of the author
First published in 2007 by Folens Limited.

ISBN-13: 978-0-00-745239-2

Julie Crimmins-Crocker asserts her moral right to be identified as the author of this work.

British Library Cataloguing in Publication Data
A catalogue record for this publication is available from the British Library.

Every effort has been made to trace copyright holders and to obtain their permission for the use of copyright material. The authors and publishers will gladly receive any information enabling them to rectify any error or omission in subsequent editions.

Managing editor: Joanne Mitchell
Layout artist: Neil Hawkins, ndesign
Illustrations: JB Illustrations, Helen Jackson and Nicola Pearce of SGA and Leonie Shearing c/o Lucas Alexander Whitley.
Cover design for this edition: Julie Martin
Design and layout for this edition: Linda Miles, Lodestone Publishing
Printed and bound in China.

Contents

This contents list provides an overview of the learning objectives of each puzzle page.

How to complete the puzzles

⭐ **1** Read the title and the instructions for each activity very carefully.

⭐ **2** For each activity, start with the simplest clues first.

⭐ **3** Crossword and wordsearch clues have numbers at the end of each clue to tell you how many letters there are in the word.

⭐ **4** If there is a word bank for you to refer to, check that your answers are in the list. Cross out the words in the word bank as you complete the clue.

⭐ **5** Use a sharp pencil at first to write down all your answers (just in case you need to change them).

⭐ **6** When you are sure your answers are correct, write them in pen or use a highlighter pen for the wordsearches.

⭐ **7** In the crosswords, write in CAPITAL LETTERS. This will make your answers easier to read.

⭐ **8** Use a dictionary and thesaurus to help you spell and find your answers.

⭐ **9** After each puzzle go to 'What's next' (page 5) and cross off the completed activity.

Remember what these useful words mean:

Synonym: the same or similar meaning, for example, ***big – large***.

Antonym: the opposite meaning, for example, ***big – small***.

Anagram: the word is muddled up, for example, **GREAL – LARGE**.

Informal: the word is simple or slang, for example, ***rabbit – bunny***.

Verbs are action and 'doing' words, for example, ***run***, ***talk*** and ***think***.

Nouns are naming words, for example, ***pen***, ***hat***, ***apple*** and ***school***.

Adjectives are describing words, for example, ***small*** bird.

Adverbs add more information to verbs, for example, *He ran* ***quickly***.

Phoneme: a letter or letters that create a single sound when said aloud, for example, **TH** and **OO**.

Letter string: a collection of phonemes, for example, **ELL**.

Vowels are the letters **a**, **e**, **i**, **o** and **u**.

Consonants are the letters of the alphabet which are <u>not</u> vowels.

What's next?

Use the answers to any of the puzzles to complete the following activities. Write down which activity you have completed and the date you did it.

	Activity	Puzzle title	Date
★1	Sort the answers into **alphabetical order**. Put them in a list.		
★2	Put the answers into **sentences** (10 sentences minimum). You can use one word per sentence or include as many words as you like in each sentence.		
★3	Put the answers into sentences that are questions. For example, *Where did my cat go?*		
★4	Put the answers into sentences that are instructions. For example, *Look after my cat when I am away.*		
★5	Put the words in the word bank into a story or piece of writing.		
★6	Write at least ten more of the same type of word.		
★7	Find **synonyms** for the words and write them down in pairs or groups. For example, *big – large, massive.*		
★8	Find **antonyms** for the words and write them down in pairs or groups. For example, *big – small, tiny, minute.*		
★9	Find **rhymes** for the words and list them. For example, *ink – sink* and *bellow – yellow, mellow* and *fellow.*		
★10	Sort the answers into groups. For example, verbs, nouns, adjectives, adverbs, number of syllables, rhyming words and so on.		
★11	Write your own new clues for the answers to a crossword, wordsearch or puzzle or create a totally new puzzle.		

Words with ACK

Word bank

SMACK
MACKEREL
SNACK
STACK
TRACK
MACKINTOSH
ATTACK
TRACKSUIT
JACKAL
JACKET
BACKWARDS
RACKET
CRACKER
HACKSAW
JACKPOT
BLACKSMITH
BACK
PACK
SHACK
RACK
SACK
BLACKBOARD
BLACK
CRACK
PACKAGE
KNACK
BACKDROP
QUACK

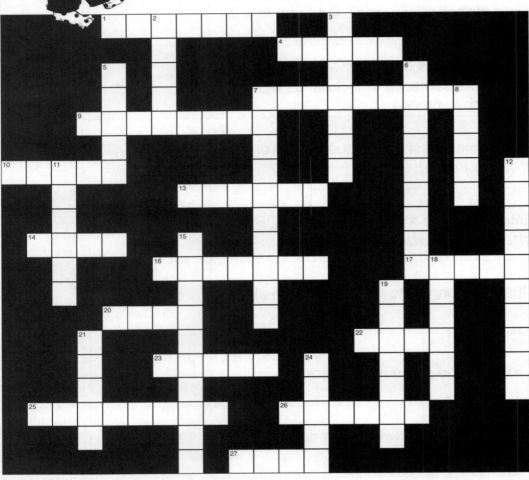

ACROSS

1. A handsaw for cutting metal (7)　**4.** The darkest colour (5)　**7.** An antonym for forwards (9)
9. An edible sea fish (8)　**10.** To hit with a flat hand (5)　**13.** A dog-like scavenging animal of Africa and Asia (6)　**14.** A large bag (4)　**16.** A parcel (7)　**17.** A trail, route or pathway (5)
20. A framework for displaying or holding things (4)　**22.** An antonym for front (4)　**23.** A small and quick meal (5)　**25.** A painted cloth behind the stage for a play (8)　**26.** A short coat (6)
27. To put clothes in bags for a holiday (4)

DOWN

2. A split or fracture (5)　**3.** The biggest prize, for example, in a lottery (7)　**5.** A pile of something (5)
6. A loose-fitting suit for athletes (9)　**7.** This is also called a chalk board (10)　**8.** A rough hut (5)
11. An antonym for defend (6)　**12.** A person who makes horseshoes and works with metal (10)
15. A waterproof raincoat (10)　**18.** You need this to play tennis (6)　**19.** A savoury biscuit eaten with cheese (7)　**21.** The noise of a duck (5)　**24.** The ability to do something or have the right technique (5)

Words with ALL

The letter string **ALL** can be pronounced in two ways, for example, *ball* and *tally*. The usual rule is that if the word ends in **ALL**, the **A** phoneme is long, for example, *netball* and *tall*. If **ALL** is in the middle or at the start of the word, the **A** phoneme is short, for example, *ballerina* and *pallet*.

Using the clues, find 10 words within this letter puzzle and circle them. The first one has been done for you. Then sort the words into two groups in the table according to their **A** phoneme.

(fall)alleyc allwallgall erynor mallyall igators hallo ww aterfallt all

1. To collapse or drop down.
2. A narrow street.
3. To speak loudly to attract attention.
4. A structure of brick or stone.
5. Where artwork is displayed.
6. Usually or typically.
7. An American animal like a crocodile.
8. Not deep.
9. A place where a river drops straight down.
10. An antonym for short.

Rhymes with STALL	Rhymes with SALLY
fall	

Now, unjumble the anagrams in brackets and put the missing words into the sentences.

1. The market _____ were covered in fruit and vegetables. (SLASTL)
2. It was hot and sunny so we _____ decided to go for a swim. (LAL)
3. The horse suddenly started to _____ and I fell off. (PLOGAL)
4. I went to the huge shopping _____ and bought everything I needed. (LAML)
5. I love _____ dancing, especially doing the waltz. (BLOMAROL)
6. On-board ship, the food is cooked in the _____. (ALGLYE)
7. I am _____ to pollen. (GALLERIC)
8. The rivers flowed down the hills into the lush green _____. (YSLEVAL)
9. I went to watch the _____ called Swan Lake. (BLEALT)
10. Beautiful stylish handwriting is also called _____. (PHIGRAYCALL)

Words with ANK

ANK can be found in many words, for example, *bankrupt, thank* and *lank*. Read the clues and use the word bank to help you to complete this wordsearch.

T	A	N	K	E	R	Q	K	B	Q	H	G	T	B	D
M	Z	M	X	J	E	N	S	H	R	A	N	K	A	T
N	Q	R	Z	L	A	E	S	T	A	N	K	R	R	K
D	B	Y	K	R	L	K	Y	T	B	K	N	T	K	T
X	F	N	F	K	R	Q	B	F	G	E	D	H	N	H
S	A	G	N	B	A	N	K	L	B	R	T	A	A	A
R	H	A	C	S	N	D	G	M	A	L	K	N	T	N
N	P	A	N	A	K	T	A	K	B	N	A	K	E	K
R	R	F	P	N	L	Q	N	N	A	W	K	N	P	F
T	V	C	D	K	Y	A	K	R	K	B	L	E	K	U
Z	A	R	H	K	T	N	P	X	D	M	Q	F	T	L
D	R	N	N	A	A	R	D	R	A	N	K	L	L	S
X	L	A	K	P	N	G	A	N	G	P	L	A	N	K
Q	R	B	S	S	K	K	L	A	N	K	Y	N	W	Y
C	Z	Z	P	R	L	K	Y	P	L	A	N	K	S	R

Word bank

BLANK	STANK
DRANK	GANGPLANK
ANKLE	TANKS
FLANK	THANK
FRANK	CRANKY
TANKER	HANKER
HANKY	SHRANK
THANKFUL	BLANKETS
LANKY	DANK
RANKLE	BANK
PRANK	PLANKS
SPANK	RANK
TANKARD	SANK

1. To continue to cause anger or bitterness (6)
2. Tall thin and bony (5)
3. A practical joke or trick (5)
4. A place where taxis wait or another word for rancid (4)
5. The side of anything (5)
6. The past tense of shrink (6)
7. A mound of earth or the edge of a river (4)
8. A large drinking cup usually for beer (7)
9. A short word for handkerchief (5)
10. To slap or smack (old-fashioned punishment) (5)
11. The past tense of stink (5)
12. To crave or long for something (6)
13. The joint between the foot and the leg (5)
14. Eccentric or bad tempered (6)
15. Thick bed covers (8)
16. Damp and chilly (4)
17. A man's name that also means outspoken, open and honest (5)
18. Grateful or appreciative (8)
19. A portable bridge to a boat (9)
20. Long flat pieces of timber (6)
21. The past tense of sink (4)
22. Without marks or writing, empty (5)
23. Storage containers for liquids or gases (5)
24. Polite people always say please and _ _ _ _ _ you (5)
25. A ship or lorry for carrying liquid (6)
26. The past tense of drink (5)

Words with ASH

ASH can be found in many words, for example, *cash*, *smash* and *rash*. When nouns that end in **ASH** become plurals, you must add **ES**, for example, *eyelash – eyelashes*.

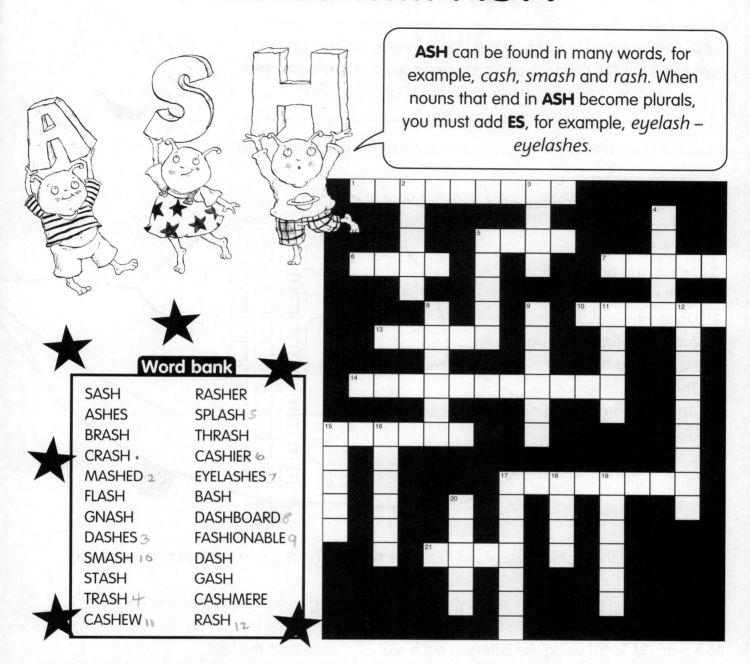

Word bank

SASH	RASHER
ASHES	SPLASH 5
BRASH	THRASH
CRASH ·	CASHIER 6
MASHED 2	EYELASHES 7
FLASH	BASH
GNASH	DASHBOARD 8
DASHES 3	FASHIONABLE 9
SMASH 10	DASH
STASH	GASH
TRASH 4	CASHMERE
CASHEW 11	RASH 12

ACROSS
1. The part of a car inside and below the windscreen (9)   **5.** A deep cut (4)   **6.** To hit violently (4)   **7.** A loud noise or car collision (5)   **10.** A type of nut (6)   **13.** A sudden burst of bright light (5)   **14.** Up to date or in the latest style (11)   **15.** To hit violently or beat soundly (6)   **17.** A fine soft fabric made from goats' wool (8)   **21.** To race or move quickly (4)

DOWN
2. To store something in a secret place (5)   **3.** An eruption of red dots on the skin (4)   **4.** To hit and break something up (5)   **5.** To grind your teeth together in anger or pain (5)   **8.** Morse code is made up of dots and _ _ _ _ _ _ (6)   **9.** To scatter liquid over something (6)   **11.** The remains of anything burnt (5)   **12.** You can put mascara on these (9)   **15.** Another word for rubbish (5)   **16.** A slice of bacon (6)   **17.** A bank clerk (7)   **18.** A decorative belt or ribbon worn around the body (4)   **19.** One way of preparing potatoes (6)   **20.** Bold and impudent (5)

Words with ELL

ELL can be found in many words, for example, *yellow*, *tell* and *smelly*. If the ELL sound is at the start of a word, it is usually spelt EL, for example, *elephant*, *elegant* and *element*.

Read the clues and write the answers for each one in the spaceship.

1. The present tense of told.
2. There are white and red ones in your blood.
3. You can ring this.
4. The past tense of fall.
5. To expand and get bigger.
6. Stinky.
7. Unhealthy or sick.
8. An underground storage room for wine perhaps.
9. The colour of lemons.
10. Another word that means goodbye.

1. E L L
2. E L L
3. E L L
4. E L L
5. E L L
6. E L L
7. E L L
8. E L L
9. E L L
10. E L L

Find and circle the eight ELL words in this letter puzzle. The first one has been done for you.

(jelly)bel lyhe llosell yells pellin gmell owin kwell

Make an ELL word using the letters in each star and write it on the line.

1. B O L W L E _____

2. S H L L E S _____

3. O R B L L E D O _____

4. G E S P L I L N _____

5. H S L L E Y J F I _____

Words with EST

When **EST** is found at the end of a word (as a suffix), it makes the word most important! For example, *most big – biggest, most loud – loudest* and *most tall – tallest*. When **EST** is added as a suffix to words ending in **Y**, the **Y** becomes an **I**, for example, *pretty – prettiest*. The suffix **EST** is not usually added to words with more than two syllables, for example, *beautiful* becomes *most beautiful*, <u>not</u> *beautifullest*.

Word bank

- CHEST
- GUEST
- ARREST
- DETEST
- DIGEST
- ESTIMATE
- LOWEST
- PEST
- CONTEST
- ESTUARY
- FASTEST
- HIGHEST
- SLOWEST
- HEAVIEST
- QUESTION
- LONGEST
- REQUEST
- BEST
- NEST
- PESTER
- REST
- TEST
- VEST
- WEST
- SUGGESTION
- INDIGESTION
- RESTAURANT

```
M P M V N K C P N Z N C M D K M N D H
E R N B K G H T V K N Z O K L T N Y E
S E M T Z T E N D Y Q B N N T T Y T A
T S F Q N B S S P E S T E R T M S Z V
U T D M J N T F T N E S T Y J E F R I
A P K J X T K S N I K T K H T W S D E
R Q P G R T E D X B M N L S M R T T S
Y R S D R W M I P M O A A O C B Q K T
L E U D O Q J G J I F F T L N T M L G
Q Q G L E Z N E T K M T T E D G J T L
P U G K M T H S W Z S G H I G H E S T
M E E F L L E T N E J N H B F N X S T
C S S D R U B S W W N Y N H Q X E S T
Q T T T Q T N O T P E B V P K B E W B
M F I Q X H L A R R E S T Y C U B T V
M F O H W S X N R X K T T D G N S F H
D I N D I G E S T I O N F X L E K T B
V E S T W X C O P Q U I P T T L N X H
R E S T A U R A N T K R F M T C J X H
```

1. A competition (7)   **2.** A sleeveless garment (4)   **3.** Someone who visits another's house (5)
4. A strong box or the upper body (5)   **5.** An antonym for answer (8)   **6.** Where people can buy and eat meals (10)   **7.** A hint or proposal (10)   **8.** To detain as the police do (6)   **9.** Where a bird lays its eggs (4)   **10.** An antonym for fastest (7)   **11.** A synonym for weightiest (8)
12. A troublesome insect or person (4)   **13.** To make an educated guess or approximation (8)
14. To really hate or despise (6)   **15.** To relax and not work is to have a _ _ _ _ (4)   **16.** To ask for something (7)   **17.** To annoy or bug someone (6)   **18.** A river mouth (7)   **19.** An antonym for worst (4)   **20.** Poor digestion or an acid stomach (11)   **21.** An antonym for highest (6)   **22.** An antonym for quickest (7)   **23.** To try something out (4)   **24.** To process food in your stomach (6)
25. An antonym for shortest (7)   **26.** An antonym for lowest (7)   **27.** An antonym for east (4)

Words with ICK

ICK can be found in many words, for example, *wicked*, *chicken* and *sickle*. With words containing more than one syllable, ICK is often spelt IC, for example, *magic*, *music* and *elastic*. Exceptions to this are *limerick* and compound words such as *lipstick*.

Using the word bank to help you, solve the clues.
Write the words in the brick wall below.

1. A type of fence usually white.
2. Difficult not easy.
3. Glue is like this.
4. The name for a set of cricket stumps.
5. Not slow.
6. A thorn or spike on a plant.
7. Walls can be made of these.
8. The part of a candle that you light.
9. An axe to use in frozen conditions.
10. A thin stream of liquid.

Word bank

WICK
ICEPICK
PICKET
TRICKLE
STICKY
WICKET
QUICK
TRICKY
BRICKS
PRICKLE

1. [ ][ ][ ][I][C][K][ ]
2. [ ][ ][ ][I][C][K]
3. [ ][ ][ ][I][C][K]
4. [ ][ ][ ][I][C][K][ ]
5. [ ][ ][ ][I][C][K]
6. [ ][ ][ ][I][C][K][ ]
7. [ ][ ][ ][I][C][K][ ]
8. [ ][ ][ ][I][C][K]
9. [ ][ ][ ][I][C][K]
10. [ ][ ][ ][ ][I][C][K][ ]

Now, find and circle the 10 ICK words in this letter puzzle.

lic k sickch icken k icking crick ettrick sthickerc licklips tickp ick

Words with ILL

ILL can be found in many words, for example, *frilly*, *sill* and *treadmill*. ILL can also be used as a prefix to mean the opposite of the root word, for example, *legible – illegible*. There are exceptions to this such as, *illuminate* and *illustrate*. When ILL is used as a prefix, the root word usually begins with L.

Word bank

ILL	CHILLY
BILL	PILLOW
HILL	GORILLA
JILL	VILLAGE
ILLEGAL	VILLAIN
FILLY	FILLET
GILLS	WINDMILL
QUILL	BRILLIANT
SILLY	MILLENIUM
STILL	ILLOGICAL
SWILL	ILLITERATE
VILLA	

ACROSS

5. Against the law (7)   **7.** Meaningless and not logical (9)   **8.** Another name for a bird's beak (4)   **9.** Put your head on one of these at night (6)   **12.** One thousand years (9)   **14.** A wicked person or criminal (7)   **17.** A boneless slice of meat or fish (6)   **20.** Unable to read or write (10)   **21.** Liquid pig food (5)   **22.** Unwell or sick (3)

DOWN

1. Weather that isn't warm may be _ _ _ _ _ _ (6)   **2.** She went up the hill with Jack in the nursery rhyme (4)   **3.** Foolish and not sensible (5)   **4.** A very small town or group of houses in the country (7)   **6.** A large ape (7)   **8.** Dazzling and wonderful (9)   **10.** A building with fanlike sails which turn in the wind (8)   **11.** An older type of large detached house (5)   **13.** A small mountain or mound of land (4)   **15.** A fish uses these for breathing (5)   **16.** A type of pen made with a feather (5)   **18.** A young female horse (5)   **19.** Stationary, not moving (5)

Words with ING

When **ING** is added to the end of a verb, the action described by the verb is continuous, for example, *I am walking today; I was walking yesterday; I will be walking tomorrow.*

Solve the clues and write the **ING** words in the word chains below. The last letter of each word is the first letter of the next word.

1. You can wear these on your fingers.
2. To tingle or feel a sharp pain.
3. The opposite of coming.
4. An antonym for taking.
5. Getting bigger or enlarging.
6. An antonym for takes.
7. A mass of small pebbles found on a beach.
8. Jewellery worn in the ears.
9. People with broken arms may wear these.
10. To speak words in tune with music.

Word bank

SING
RINGS
SLINGS
EARRINGS
SHINGLE
BRINGS
GROWING
GOING
GIVING
STING

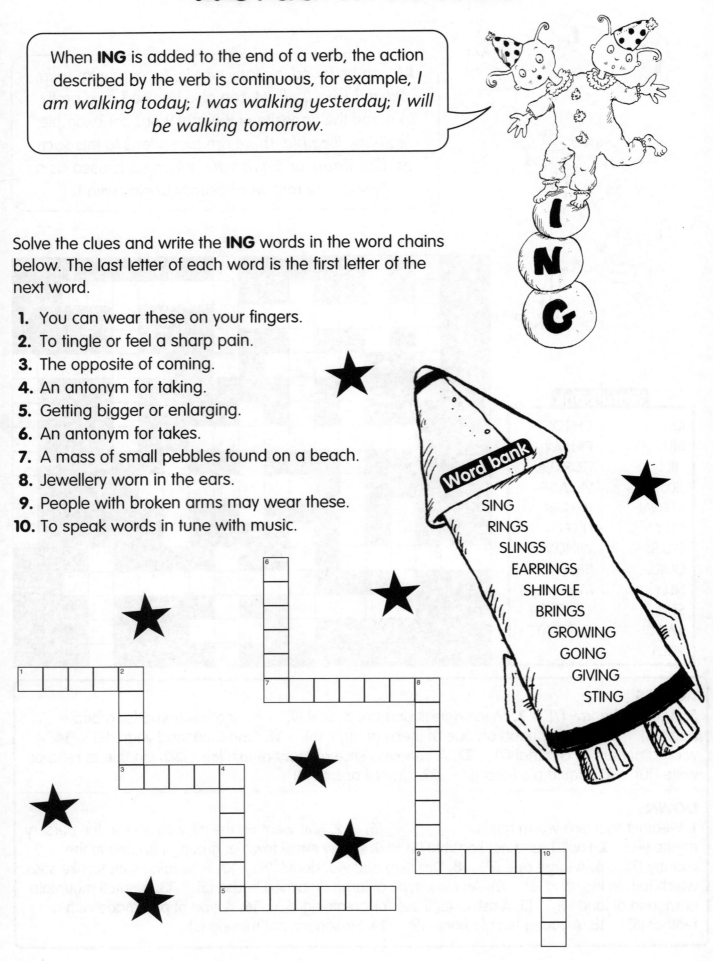

Words with ING

Write these **ING** words in the sentences below, so that they make sense.

Word bank

MOVING	SING	OPENING	MINGLE
WATCHING	MAKING	LOOKING	FINGERS
DRIVING	JOKING	KING	
	WRING	SPEAKING	
	DING	PACKING	
	DRESSING	TINGLE	
	JINGLE	INGOTS	
	COOKING	SINGLE	
	DIVING	EATING	

1. As I was __ __ __ __ __ __ __ a cake, I heard the doorbell go __ __ __ __ dong.

2. The children were __ __ __ __ __ __ into the sea and __ __ __ __ __ __ __ __ for shells in the sand.

3. The __ __ __ __ and queen were __ __ __ __ __ __ __ to a new palace, so they were __ __ __ __ __ __ __ __ all their gold __ __ __ __ __ __.

4. At the banquet, people were __ __ __ __ __ __ wonderful food while laughing and __ __ __ __ __ __ with their friends.

5. At my birthday party, I had to __ __ __ __ __ __ __ with all the guests and make sure that the __ __ __ __ __ __ people on their own weren't left out.

6. Yesterday morning as I was __ __ __ __ __ __ __ __ __ for school, I heard a __ __ __ __ __ __ __ on the radio advertising a new breakfast cereal.

7. Because I forgot my gloves, my __ __ __ __ __ __ __ were freezing and when I warmed them up they began to __ __ __ __ __ __.

8. When my dad is in the kitchen __ __ __ __ __ __ __ he doesn't like anyone __ __ __ __ __ __ __ __ him, especially if he is secretly __ __ __ __ __ __ __ packet meals from the supermarket.

9. The band began to __ __ __ __ their latest song, but everyone was __ __ __ __ __ __ __ __ and not listening to the music.

10. It was a really wet day and I had to __ __ __ __ __ the water out of my skirt after a car that was __ __ __ __ __ __ __ by splashed me.

Words with INK

Example of **INK** words are *chink*, *wrinkled* and *stink*. There are only a few words that begin with **INK**, for example, *inkwell* and *inkling*. At the start of words, usually it is written **INC**, for example, *incline* and *include*.

ACROSS

5. To swallow liquid (5)   **6.** Boisterous merry making is called high _ _ _ _ _ (5)   **8.** To give off a nasty smell (5)   **11.** To go fishing you need a hook, line and _ _ _ _ _ _ (6)   **13.** A fur coat may be made of this (4)   **14.** A small ornament (7)   **16.** To quickly open and close one eye (4)   **18.** A connection or a ring of a chain (4)   **19.** A tight twist in wire or rope (4)   **20.** To get smaller, as clothes sometimes do when washed (6)

DOWN

1. The edge of a steep place (5)   **2.** A hint or vague idea (7)   **3.** To sneak or move stealthily (5)   **4.** To meddle or mess with (6)   **7.** To scatter small drops (8)   **8.** An antonym for float (4)   **9.** The fluid used in pens (3)   **10.** To open and close your eyes (5)   **12.** You get these on your face as you get older (8)   **15.** To use your brain (5)   **17.** A slang word for tiny (5)

Word bank

INK	SINK
KINK	INKLING
DRINK	DINKY
LINK	JINKS
WRINKLES	SLINK
MINK	STINK
WINK	THINK
SPRINKLE	SHRINK
BLINK	TINKER
BRINK	TRINKET

Words with OCK

OCK can be found in many words, for example, *smock*, *dreadlocks* and *pocket*. At the start of a word, it is spelt **OC** not **OCK**, for example, *October*, *occupy* and *occasion*.

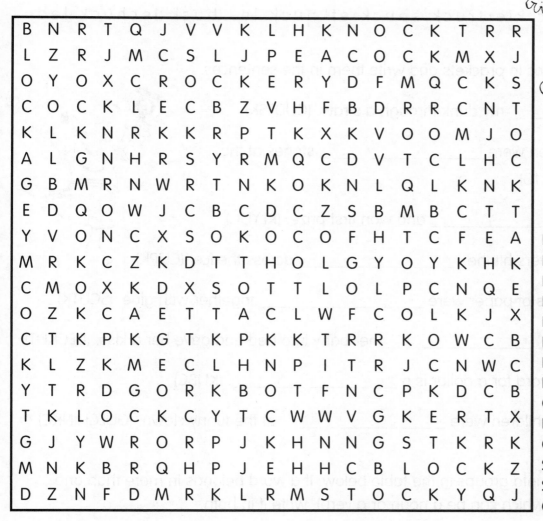

```
B N R T Q J V V K L H K N O C K T R R
L Z R J M C S L J P E A C O C K M X J
O Y O X C R O C K E R Y D F M Q C K S
C O C K L E C B Z V H F B D R R C N T
K L K N R K K R P T K X K V O O M J O
A L G N H R S Y R M Q C D V T C L H C
G B M R N W R T N K O K N L Q L K N K
E D Q O W J C B C D C Z S B M B C T T
Y V O N C X S O K O C O F H T C F E A
M R K C Z K D T T H O L G Y O Y K H K
C M O X K D X S O T T L O L P C N Q E
O Z K C A E T T A C L W F C O L K J X
C T K P K G T K P K K T R R K O W C B
K L Z K M E C L H N P I T R J C N W C
Y T R D G O R K B O T F N C P K D C B
T K L O C K C Y T C W W V G K E R T X
G J Y W R O R P J K H N N G S T K R K
M N K B R Q H P J E H H C B L O C K Z
D Z N F D M R K L R M S T O C K Y Q J
```

Word bank

PADDOCK	LOCKET
PEACOCK	ROCKET
ROCKERY	STOCKY
BLOCKAGE	SHOCK
FROCK	SOCKS
HADDOCK	STOCK
KNOCKER	DOCK
KNOCK	LOCK
COCKLE	MOCK
DOCKET	ROCK
CROCKERY	TOCK
STOCKINGS	BLOCK
STOCKTAKE	CLOCK
COCKATOO	COCKY

1. A garden with stones (7)   **2.** A type of firework that flies upwards very fast (6)   **3.** These are worn by ladies on their legs and can be made of nylon or silk (9)   **4.** You can tell the time with this (5)   **5.** The sound of a clock 'tick _ _ _ _ ' (4)   **6.** A man-made harbour for loading or unloading ships (4)   **7.** Distress or injury caused by electricity (5)   **8.** A ticket or bill sent with a package (6)   **9.** A bird with a beautiful fanlike tail (7)   **10.** A count up or valuation of goods in a store (9)   **11.** Arrogant or big headed (5)   **12.** A solid rectangular piece of wood or stone (5)   **13.** Dishes and plates (8)   **14.** You can put your key in this (4)   **15.** A stone or boulder (4)   **16.** A woman's dress (5)   **17.** You wear these on your feet inside your shoes (5)   **18.** A small crested parrot (8)   **19.** If there is no door bell, you may use a _ _ _ _ _ _ _ (7)   **20.** An edible shellfish (6)   **21.** To ridicule or laugh at (4)   **22.** An obstruction (8)   **23.** Things stored for sale or later use (5)   **24.** A type of fish (7)   **25.** A small hinged pendant (6)   **26.** A field or grass enclosure (7)   **27.** Chunky or thickset (6)   **28.** To strike or rap (on a door perhaps) (5)

Words with UCK

UCK can be found in many words, for example, *ruck*, *yucky* and *sucker*.

Find and circle the eight words in this letter puzzle. The first one has been done for you.

d u c k m u c k y l u c k i e r t r u c k s b u c k e t k n u c k l e s b u c k l e c h u c k l e d

Unjumble the anagrams in brackets and write them in the sentences.

1. I _____ my drink through a straw. (CUDESK)

2. The naughty children were _____ stones at the windows. (INCKCHUG)

3. I was really _____ and won first prize. (KLYUC)

4. The ice hockey players hit the _____ across the ice. (CUPK)

5. The pieces of paper were _____ together with glue. (SCUTK)

6. The lady _____ her baby into bed and gave her a kiss. (DECKUT)

7. A slang word for a dollar is a _____. (KUBC)

8. The little children were _____ at the funny clown. (GULCHINKC)

Sort these **UCK** words into groups in the table below. If a word belongs in more than one group, such as *duck* (which can be a noun or a verb), write it in both.

★ plucky   duckling   suck   truck   luckily   knuckle   tucked   plucking   buckle   mucky   chuckle   stuck   bucket ★

Verb	Noun	Adverb	Adjective

Words with UMP

UMP can be found in many words, for example, *jumpy* and *chump*. Read the clues and use the word bank to help you to complete this crossword.

Word bank

BUMP	THUMP
DUMP	FRUMPY
LUMP	GRUMPY
PUMP	RUMPLE
RUMP	STUMPY
CLUMP	CRUMPET
DUMPY	CRUMPLE
HUMPS	TRUMPET
LUMPY	HUMPBACK
MUMPS	DUMPLINGS
PLUMP	SUMPTUOUS
SLUMP	SCRUMPTIOUS
STUMP	

ACROSS

3. Dowdy and old fashioned (6)   **6.** A disease which causes swelling in the neck (5)   **8.** The tail or rear end of something (4)   **9.** The remains of chopped down tree (5)   **10.** To crease or crunch up (7)   **11.** Lavish or magnificent (9)   **12.** Short and stout (5)   **14.** A lump or swelling (4)   **19.** A shapeless mass (4)   **20.** A flat soft cake eaten toasted with butter (7)   **21.** Rounded and not skinny (5)   **22.** Small doughy puddings eaten with stew (9)

DOWN

1. Bad tempered and unhappy (6)   **2.** Use this to put air in a ball or tyre (4)   **4.** To strike or hit heavily (5)   **5.** A metal musical instrument that you blow (7)   **7.** To collapse or fall heavily (5)   **10.** A cluster of plants (5)   **11.** Delicious and good to eat (11)   **13.** A type of whale (8)   **15.** A rubbish heap (4)   **16.** A camel can have one or two of these (5)   **17.** To make untidy or dishevelled (6)   **18.** Short and thickset (6)   **19.** Uneven and not smooth, like porridge perhaps (5)

Words with UNK

Examples of **UNK** words are *punk* and *shrunken*. At the start of a word, it is spelt **UNC** not **UNK**. This is because the root words begin with **C** and have the prefix **UN**, for example, *unclear* and *uncanny*.

Find and circle the eight words with **UNK** in this letter puzzle. The first one has been done for you.

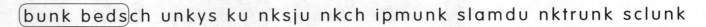

(bunk beds)ch unkys ku nksju nkch ipmunk slamdu nktrunk sclunk

Using the clues, circle or highlight the **UNK** words in the wordsearch below.

1. A small North American animal that can smell awful (5)
2. A person who has had too much alcohol (5)
3. The past tense of stink (5)
4. Divers sometimes search the seabed for _ _ _ _ _ _ treasure (6)
5. To fail an exam or test (5)
6. To dip bread or a biscuit in liquid before eating (4)
7. The sound of metal being hit (5)

8. A storage container or a sandy hollow on a golf course (6)
9. A thick solid piece (of wood perhaps) (5)
10. The past tense of shrink (6)
11. A small striped North American animal (8)
12. Two single beds, one on top of the other (8)
13. A thick piece (of bread perhaps) (4)
14. Useless objects or a name for fast food (4)
15. An elephant has one of these (5)

L	K	M	C	B	H	H	V	J	R	N
D	P	T	C	H	L	V	X	W	T	F
S	R	F	H	Z	I	W	J	N	R	L
T	N	U	U	K	T	P	R	U	U	U
U	B	X	N	E	T	E	M	Y	N	N
N	C	U	K	K	K	P	N	U	K	K
K	K	V	N	N	K	E	H	U	N	K
S	I	B	U	N	K	B	E	D	S	K
P	B	B	U	N	C	T	L	J	K	L
M	N	L	U	Q	S	H	R	U	N	K
T	C	S	H	Z	D	U	N	K	L	N

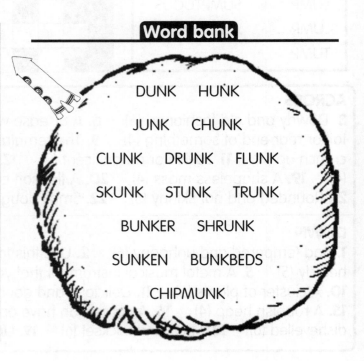

Word bank

DUNK   HUNK

JUNK   CHUNK

CLUNK   DRUNK   FLUNK

SKUNK   STUNK   TRUNK

BUNKER   SHRUNK

SUNKEN   BUNKBEDS

CHIPMUNK

Words that end in A or O

These words all end in **A** or **O**. This is not a common ending for English words and many of them originate in other countries, for example, *patio* and *vanilla* are Spanish words, while *pizza* and *risotto* are Italian. Notice that with all these words, the emphasis is not usually on the final syllable.

Join these words to the correct **A** or **O** ending and write them on the line below. One has been done for you.

A **O**

VISA	VIDE_	PAST_	RADI_	POTAT_	TOMAT_	VILL_	PANORAM_

VISA _____

Unjumble the anagrams in brackets and write them in the sentences below.

1. The Leaning Tower of _____ can be found in Italy. (SAIP)

2. The _____ is a furry mammal found in _____. (DANAP, INCHA)

3. The _____ is an extinct bird which was the size of a turkey and couldn't fly. (DOOD)

4. _____ is a game in which numbers are called out and you have to cross them off your card. (GIBNO)

5. The ship was carrying a heavy _____ when it sank. (CROAG)

6. _____ is one of the countries in the continent of Asia. (IDINA)

7. I called out my name in the cave and I heard an _____ call back at me. (HOCE)

8. In a rainbow, the colour between blue and violet is _____. (GINDOI)

Write these words next to the clue they are connected to.

	POLO	VANILLA	LEO	DUO	STEREO	
★	HYSTERIA	SOLO	HALO	BONGO	VERTIGO	★

1. Crazy laughter _____

2. Two people _____

3. An angel _____

4. Lion _____

5. Ice cream _____

6. Drums _____

7. A ball game _____

8. Two speakers _____

9. One _____

10. Giddiness _____

Words that end in EE or OO

These words all end in the phonemes **EE** or **OO**. When words with **OO** have more than one syllable, the emphasis is usually on the final syllable, for example, *hullabaloo*. Most one-syllable words that end in the **EE** phoneme are spelt with **EE**, exceptions to this rule are *me*, *be*, *she* and *he*.

Word bank

KANGAROO	BOO
CUCKOO	SPREE
TOFFEE	TREE
GLEE	COFFEE
DEGREE	ZOO
AGREE	THREE
PEDIGREE	TEPEE
IGLOO	LOO
REFEREE	FREE
FEE	FLEE
DIDGERIDOO	WEE
BEE	SEE
TOO	KNEE
TABOO	GEE

ACROSS

3. A bird that lays its eggs in others' nests (6)   **7.** Unit of measurement for temperature or angles (6)   **9.** An umpire or adjudicator (7)   **14.** To say yes or have the same opinion (5)   **15.** An expression of surprise or amazement '_ _ _ whiz!' (3)   **17.** Something forbidden or banned (5)   **18.** An Australian Aboriginal instrument (10)   **19.** A Native American cone-shaped tent (5)   **20.** The cost charged for a service (3)   **21.** You use your eyes to do this (3)   **22.** A large plant with a woody trunk (4)   **23.** Polite slang for a toilet (3)   **24.** A loud exclamation made to scare someone (3)

DOWN

1. A place to see animals from all over the world (3)   **2.** A session of over indulgence, for example, 'To go on a shopping _ _ _ _ _' (5)   **3.** A hot drink made from roasted, ground beans (6)   **4.** The leg joint between thigh and calf (4)   **5.** Small or tiny (3)   **6.** A register of ancestors or a pure breed of animal (8)   **8.** Cheerfulness or joy (4)   **10.** To run away and not fight (4)   **11.** An insect that makes honey (3)   **12.** A dome-shaped house made from snow (5)   **13.** Australian marsupial with strong hind legs for jumping (8)   **16.** Not costing anything or no longer in jail (4)   **17.** A chewy sweet (6)   **19.** 2 + 1 (5)   **22.** Also or as well (3)

Plural nouns with ES

To make singular nouns into plurals, we often just add **S**, but for nouns that end in **SS**, **CH**, **SH** and **X** we must add **ES**, for example, *kiss – kisses*, *tax – taxes*, *cockroach – cockroaches* and *bush – bushes*. Make the ten nouns below into plurals and, on a separate piece of paper, sort them into two groups: 'Just add **S**' and 'Add **ES**'.

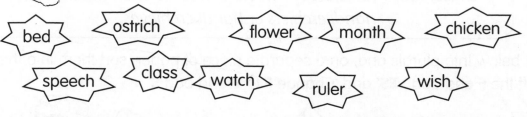

bed | ostrich | flower | month | chicken | speech | class | watch | ruler | wish

Word bank

KISS
DRESS
ADDRESS
CROSS
FOX
CHURCH
SANDWICH
BUNCH
MATCH
PATCH
BEACH
SCRATCH
STITCH
DISH
BRUSH
CRASH
TOOTHBRUSH
ASH
WITCH
BENCH
BOX

Read the clues and add **ES** to the words in the word bank to complete this crossword.

ACROSS

1. An artist uses these to paint with (7) **6.** Girls and women wear these (7) **9.** You see lots of these in graveyards (7) **10.** You can sit on these (7) **11.** I made lots of these for my picnic lunch (10) **14.** Dangerous roads have many car _ _ _ _ _ _ _ (7) **16.** I had lots of these when I fell into the brambles (9) **17.** These are useful to start a fire with (7) **18.** These are great for cleaning teeth (12) **19.** A synonym for plates and bowls (6) **20.** Women with black pointy hats and broomsticks (7)

DOWN

1. Groups of flowers tied together (7) **2.** You write these on envelopes (9) **3.** These have sand and shells on them (7) **4.** Farmers don't like these animals as they kill their chickens (5) **5.** I put these on the bottom of my letters to my granny (6) **7.** Bad cuts are sewn up with these (8) **8.** Christian religious buildings (8) **12.** These are used to mend old clothes (7) **13.** Containers (5) **15.** These are left after a fire has gone out (5)

Plural nouns when F changes to VES

To change singular nouns into plurals we usually just add **S**, but this isn't always the case. For nouns that end in **F**, we change the **F** to **V** and add **ES**, for example, *wharf – wharves*. For nouns that end in **FE**, we change the **F** to **V** and add **S**, for example, *life – lives*. There are a few exceptions to this rule, for example, *belief – beliefs, chief – chiefs, roof – roofs, hoof – hoofs or hooves* and *handkerchief – handkerchiefs or handkerchieves*.

Make the ten nouns below into plurals and, on a separate piece of paper, sort them into the two groups: 'Take off the **F** and add **VES**' and 'Change **F** to **V** and add **S**'.

yourself

shelf

elf

knife

leaf

wife

wolf

calf

life

thief

Change the words in the word bank into plurals to make your answers, then read the sentences below. Highlight the missing plurals in the wordsearch and write them in the gaps.

1. In the winter, we wear _ _ _ _ _ _ _ around our necks to keep warm. (7)

2. In the bakery there were many _ _ _ _ _ _ of bread. (6)

3. The _ _ _ _ _ _ and the fairies played in the secret garden. (5)

4. The mother cows were looking for their _ _ _ _ _ _. (6)

5. There are two _ _ _ _ _ _ in a whole. (6)

6. They say a cat has nine _ _ _ _ _. (5)

7. The boats were moored up against the _ _ _ _ _ _ _. (7)

S	C	A	R	V	E	S	T
W	N	H	N	K	S	D	C
Z	H	V	E	E	L	S	A
J	K	A	V	L	E	D	L
Z	L	A	R	V	V	Z	V
N	O	H	L	V	P	E	E
L	B	A	N	X	E	G	S
M	H	L	I	V	E	S	M

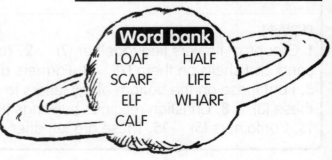

Word bank

LOAF   HALF

SCARF   LIFE

ELF   WHARF

CALF

Plural nouns when Y changes to IES

To make singular nouns into plurals, we usually just add **S**, but this isn't always the case. For nouns that end in a consonant then **Y**, we change the **Y** to **I** and add **ES**, for example, *baby – babies* and *tummy – tummies*.

Write down the singular version for the plural nouns below. The first one has been done for you.

Plural	Singular
berries	*berry*
ladies	
flies	
puppies	
jellies	

Plural	Singular
families	
parties	
memories	
cherries	
cities	

Change the nouns in the word bank into plurals to make your answers. Read the clues and write the answers in the crossword.

Word bank

CITY	MYSTERY
PONY	BOUNDARY
PARTY	BUTTERFLY
CAVITY	DICTIONARY
QUARRY	FAIRY
FACTORY	HOBBY

ACROSS
2. At the riding stables there are lots of these (6)   8. You will see these on industrial estates (9)
9. These are a like open cast mines (8)   10. Fences and walls mark these (10)   11. These books have words and their definitions in them (12)   12. These are strange events that cannot be explained (9)

DOWN
1. These are pastimes such as stamp collecting (7)   3. These mythical female creatures have wings (7)   4. London is one of the largest _ _ _ _ _ _ in the world (6)   5. Caterpillars turn into these (11)   6. Many people have these to celebrate birthdays and special occasions (7)
7. A dentist drills and fills these holes in teeth (8)

Plural nouns when Y stays the same and S is added

Sometimes when nouns end in **Y** we do not need to change the **Y** and we can just add **S** to make a plural. This is only the case when the **Y** follows a vowel, for example, *day – days* and *valley – valleys*.

Change the nouns in the word bank into plurals to make your answers. The nouns in this crossword all have a vowel before the **Y**. Write the plural forms in the crossword.

ACROSS
3. They use lots of these in a hairdressing salon (10)
6. Planes taxi and take off along these (7)
7. Young men of school age (4)
9. Hills go up and these go down (7)
10. A synonym for routes or directions (4)
11. There are seven of these in a week (4)
12. At the cats' and dogs' home there are lots of these (6)

DOWN
1. These medical photographs show if your bones are broken (5)
2. There are lots of these at the art gallery (8)
4. Smokers put their cigarette ash in these (8)
5. These people have been stranded on desert islands (9)
8. These are performed in theatres (5)

Word bank

VALLEY
BOY
DAY
RUNWAY
ASHTRAY
PLAY
CASTAWAY
XRAY
HAIRSPRAY
WAY
DISPLAY
STRAY

Plural nouns

The answers to this crossword are plural nouns. They are regular plurals that follow the rules. Add **S** to most words, for example, *bag – bags* and *cake – cakes*. Add **ES** to words that end in **S**, **CH** and **SH**, for example, *pass – passes*, *church – churches* and *bush – bushes*. Change **F** to **VES**, for example, *wife – wives*. Change **Y** after a consonant to **IES**, for example, *fly – flies*.

Read the clues and make the nouns in the word bank into plurals to find the answers in this crossword.

Word bank

CAR	LEAF
DAY	ANIMAL
EGG	CRASH
BUS	JELLY
SOCK	MATCH
SPY	PUPPY
TREE	WATCH
BABY	WINDOW
HOOF	BALLOON
KNIFE	BRANCH
LADY	BIRTHDAY
LASH	SUITCASE

ACROSS

3. Your wear these on your feet inside your shoes (5)
6. These can be found in zoos (7)
11. We celebrate these once a year when we become a year older (9)
12. These are blown up and can go 'pop!' (8)
14. Fruit-flavoured desserts eaten at parties (7)
16. Another word for women (6)
17. Large plants with trunks (5)
19. Leaves grow on these (8)
20. You can use these to light a fire (7)
21. Young dogs (7)
22. Hens lay these (4)
23. Openings in buildings made of glass (7)

DOWN

1. You'll need to pack these for a holiday (9)
2. People wear these on their wrists to tell the time (7)
3. They sneak around watching people (5)
4. There are lots of these on the roads (4)
5. There are seven of these in a week (4)
7. They are green and they grow on trees (6)
8. Horses have these on their feet (6)
9. Passengers can travel in these on the roads (5)
10. Collisions between cars (7)
13. Sharp tools found in the kitchen (6)
15. Hairs that grow on your eyelids (6)
18. Very young children (6)

The prefixes AUTO and BI

The prefixes **AUTO** and **BI** all provide additional information about the words that follow them. **AUTO** comes from the Greek word **AUTOS** which means 'self'. For example, a **bi**ography is the story of one person's life written by someone else, but an **auto**biography is the story of a person's life written by him or herself.

In the tables below there are some missing words and some missing definitions. Write them in the spaces. You may use a dictionary to help.

AUTO – word	Definition
	A person's signature.
autonomy	
	The device on a plane that enables it to fly itself.
automaton	
	The personal inspection of a person's dead body.

BI comes from the Latin words **BIS** and **BINI** which mean 'twice' or 'two'. For example, **bi**cycle means 'a cycle with **two** wheels'.

BI – word	Definition
biannual	
	Once in two months.
	A swimming costume with two parts.
bivalve	
	Able to speak two languages.

The prefixes AUTO and BI

The answers to these clues all begin with **AUTO** or **BI**. Read the clues carefully, then write the words in the crossword. Use the word bank to help you.

Word bank

AUTOMATIC
AUTOMOBILE
AUTOMATION
AUTOGYRO
AUTONYM
AUTOCRAT
AUTOSUGGESTION
BIFOCAL
BICENTENARY
BINOCULARS
BISECT
BINARY
BIPED
BIPLANE
BIWEEKLY
BILATERAL
BIANNUAL

ACROSS

1. An animal with **two** feet (5)
2. A system of numbers with only **two** digits – 0 and 1 (6)
4. Occurring once every **two** years or twice a year (8)
6. Occurring once every **two** weeks or twice a week (8)
7. A self-propelled rotating wing aircraft with an unpowered rotor (8)
8. To divide into **two** parts (6)
9. Having two sides or **two** parties involved (9)
12. A motor car (self-propelled) (10)
13. The introduction of machines and mechanical processes in industry (10)
14. A leader who rules on his own, an absolute sovereign (8)
15. Lenses with **two** parts for near and far vision (7)

DOWN

1. **200th** anniversary (11)
2. You can see into the distance with these (like **two** telescopes joined together) (10)
3. Writing published under the author's real name (7)
5. A mental process originating in a person's own mind (14)
10. Controlled mechanically without thinking or for a weapon, self loading (9)
11. A plane or glider with **two** sets of wings (7)

The prefixes CIRCUM, TELE and TRANS

The prefixes **CIRCUM**, **TELE** and **TRANS** all provide additional information about the words that follow them. **CIRCUM** comes from a Latin word meaning 'about' or 'around'. For example, *circumference* means 'boundary' and is most commonly used to describe the distance around the edge of a circle. **TELE** comes from a Greek word meaning 'far' or 'distant'. For example, *teleconference* means a 'conference' or 'meeting' carried out by people who are far apart. **TRANS** comes from a Latin word meaning 'across' or 'beyond'. For example, *transatlantic* means 'across' or 'beyond' the Atlantic Ocean.

Find and circle the five **CIRCUM** words in this puzzle. Use a dictionary to find out what they mean and, on a separate piece of paper, put them into sentences.

ci rcum stan ces c ircu mspec tcir cum vent cir cumstan tialcircum navig ate

Match the **TELE** words with the words on the lines below and rephrase.

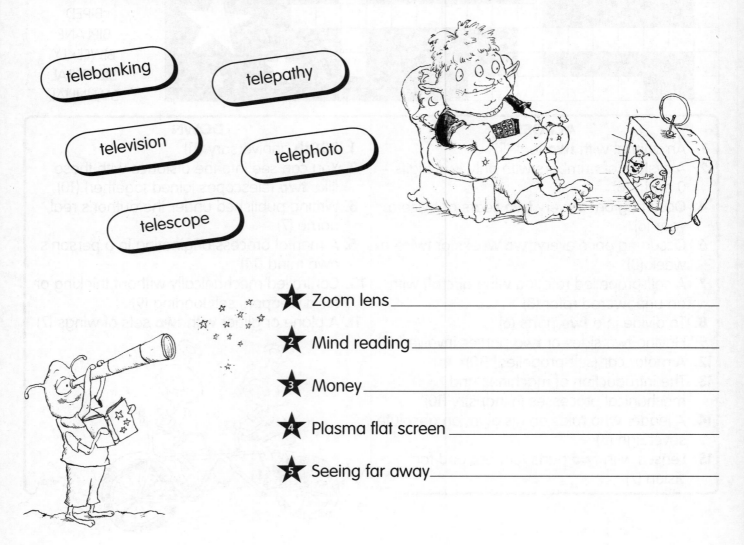

telebanking   telepathy

television   telephoto

telescope

⭐ **1** Zoom lens_____

⭐ **2** Mind reading_____

⭐ **3** Money_____

⭐ **4** Plasma flat screen_____

⭐ **5** Seeing far away_____

The prefixes CIRCUM, TELE and TRANS

The answers to the clues are all words beginning with **TRANS**. Find them in the wordsearch.

```
L T R A N S C E N D L T J
T T T K W R J D R T R R T
R R T R M F B X N K N A R
A T A H A C L A M O R N A
N L R N G N L Z I B D S N
S T P R S P S T P R L F S
C R V N S L C P E F R U F
R H N N L A A F O N Q S O
I X A K S Z S T W R M I R
P R L N T N Y O P T O M
T K A D A T N Y N R R N F
G R T R A N S P A R E N T
T J T T R A N S I S T O R
```

1. To rise above (9)
2. To send from one person or one place to another (8)
3. A written copy or report of a conversation (10)
4. Cars buses and trains are all forms of this (9)
5. Another word for 'see-through' (11)
6. To transfer a human organ from one person to another (10)
7. A single sale or purchase (11)
8. An old fashioned type of portable radio (10)
9. Someone who interprets from one language to another (10)
10. To transfer blood into an ill person (11)
11. To change shape or character (9)

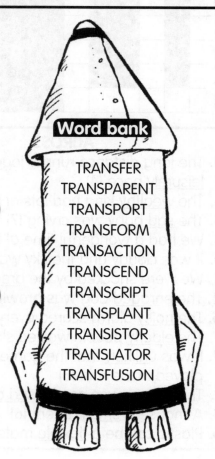

Word bank

TRANSFER
TRANSPARENT
TRANSPORT
TRANSFORM
TRANSACTION
TRANSCEND
TRANSCRIPT
TRANSPLANT
TRANSISTOR
TRANSLATOR
TRANSFUSION

Adjectives

Adjectives describe (in more detail) what nouns are like, for example, *a **rough** sea*, *a **sharp** knife* and *a **wicked** queen*.

> The answers to this crossword are all adjectives. To work out what they are, replace the underlined words in the clues with similar adjectives. You can use the word bank to help you.

Word bank

ANGRY	BUMPY
TALL	LOUD
OLD	PRETTY
BENDY	UGLY
AWFUL	PALE
GREAT	GREY
UNHAPPY	PROUD
LITTLE	SWEET
DEAD	RICH
TINY	SLOW
WRIGGLY	HELPFUL
SHY	CHEERFUL
FLUFFY	ORANGE
DOUBTFUL	

ACROSS

1. The long distance runner jogged at a <u>leisurely</u> pace (4)
4. The <u>wealthy</u> king had lots of money (4)
6. The <u>sad</u> baby was crying (7)
8. We had a <u>wonderful</u> time at the zoo (5)
10. It was cloudy and the sky was <u>dull</u> (4)
12. We were shocked by the <u>dreadful</u> news (5)
14. The <u>enraged</u> dog was growling (5)
15. The <u>noisy</u> alarm scared everyone (4)
17. The <u>elderly</u> people walked slowly (3)
19. It was <u>unlikely</u> that the game would be played in the rain (8)
22. The winner was <u>as pleased as punch</u> (5)
24. A mouse is <u>small</u> rodent (6)
25. Plastic can be a <u>flexible</u> material (5)

DOWN

1. The <u>timid</u> boy spoke quietly (3)
2. The <u>squirming</u> worm was on the path (7)
3. The road was <u>smooth</u> (5)
5. The <u>happy</u> children were laughing (8)
7. The princess was very <u>beautiful</u> (6)
9. Some basketball players are six feet <u>high</u> (4)
11. The diamond was very expensive but <u>minute</u> (4)
13. The baby loved the <u>soft</u> toys (6)
16. The nurse was very <u>supportive</u> (7)
18. Some rare animals are now all <u>extinct</u> (4)
20. The fruit was a <u>reddish-yellow</u> colour (6)
21. The dessert was really <u>sugary</u> (5)
22. The patient's skin was <u>white and pasty</u> (4)
23. The monster was <u>hideous</u> to look at (4)

Adverbs

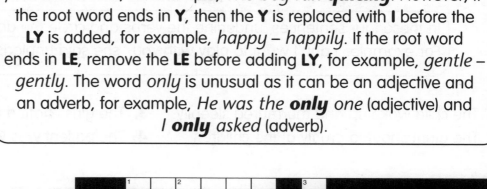

Adverbs describe how the verb is performed and they usually end in **LY**. The suffix **LY** can be added directly to most words, for example, *The boy ran **quickly***. However, if the root word ends in **Y**, then the **Y** is replaced with **I** before the **LY** is added, for example, *happy – happily*. If the root word ends in **LE**, remove the **LE** before adding **LY**, for example, *gentle – gently*. The word *only* is unusual as it can be an adjective and an adverb, for example, *He was the **only** one* (adjective) and *I **only** asked* (adverb).

To find the answers in this crossword, replace the underlined word or words with an adverb similar in meaning. Use the word bank to help you.

Word bank

LOUDLY	SECURELY	LATELY
YEARLY	PROUDLY	ICILY
HAPPILY	PLAINLY	BUSILY
FINELY	CLEARLY	LASTLY
LIGHTLY	NICELY	LAZILY
DEFINITELY	DIMLY	
CAREFULLY	SHYLY	

ACROSS

1. He worked <u>briskly and industriously</u> (6)   **5.** The climbers moved <u>cautiously</u> up the cliff (9)
7. The judge spoke very <u>coldly</u> to the prisoner (5)   **8.** The mountain could be <u>plainly</u> seen in the distance (7)   **9.** The food should be <u>delicately</u> seasoned (7)   **10.** The cat stretched <u>slowly and sleepily</u> (6)   **11.** The dark room was <u>poorly</u> lit (5)   **13.** The teacher explained the problem <u>simply</u> (7)   **16.** The lion roared <u>noisily</u> (6)   **17.** The fair took place <u>annually</u> (6)

DOWN

2. The jewels were locked away <u>safely</u> (8)   **3.** The children played <u>cheerfully</u> (7)   **4.** The quiet little girl spoke <u>timidly</u> (5)   **6.** It has been too cold <u>recently</u> for swimming (6)   **11.** Rough water is <u>certainly</u> risky for swimming (10)   **12.** And <u>finally</u>, we should say thanks and goodbye (6)   **13.** The artist displayed his work with <u>pride</u> (7)   **14.** Children should always speak <u>politely</u> to others (6)
15. The violin was <u>skilfully</u> tuned (6)

Dialogue adverbs

The answers to these puzzles are dialogue adverbs that describe how something is said. They all end in **LY**, for example, *The boy spoke **sadly** about his broken toy.*

In these four sentences, underline the verbs and circle the adverbs. For example, 'I don't want to play with you,' she <u>said</u> (unpleasantly).

1. The child woke up and murmured sleepily.

2. The giant shouted gruffly at the children.

3. The girls chatted merrily about the party.

4. The patient was weak and mumbled faintly.

The dialogue adverbs in this crossword have two syllables, for example, *I speak French very **badly**.* Read the clues and think about which adverbs could describe the dialogue in them. Use the word bank to help you. Write your answers in the crossword.

Word bank

BRAVELY	FIERCELY
CLEARLY	QUICKLY
CALMLY	SOFTLY
LOUDLY	GRIMLY
KINDLY	PROUDLY

ACROSS

7. 'I didn't do it. It wasn't me,' the angry child shouted _ _ _ _ _ _ _ _. (8)

8. When the fire alarm went off, the teacher spoke _ _ _ _ _ _ and said that we must leave the classroom. (6)

9. The athlete talked _ _ _ _ _ _ _ about his medals. (7)

10. The football referee spoke _ _ _ _ _ _ so he could be heard. (6)

DOWN

1. The mother murmured _ _ _ _ _ _ to her baby. (6)

2. The policeman asked _ _ _ _ _ _ if I was lost.(6)

3. He announced _ _ _ _ _ _ _, 'I will climb the mountain and rescue the man.' (7)

4. 'Speak _ _ _ _ _ _ _. We are in a hurry,' I said. (7)

5. The fireman commented _ _ _ _ _ _ that someone had died in the fire. (6)

6. The winner of the speech competition spoke very _ _ _ _ _ _ _. (7)

Dialogue adverbs

Dialogue adverbs describe how something is said. The dialogue adverbs in this wordsearch have three syllables, for example, *The actors spoke so* **rapidly** *that we couldn't understand them.* Read the clues and unjumble the anagrams to find the adverbs. Then find and circle the adverbs in the wordsearch.

1. The young actor uttered his lines REVSONLUY. (9)
2. The farmer yelled LIGRANY, 'Get off my land!' (7)
3. 'It is good fun to run in front of cars,' the boy called out SHYLOFOLI. (9)
4. The contestants answered each question slowly and CREFLALUY. (9)
5. The girl replied GLEAREY that she would play in the team. (7)
6. The children chattered ISLINOY. (7)

7. The little girl was shy and spoke DIMILYT. (7)
8. 'Today is my birthday,' the boy announced FLYUHCLEER. (10)
9. '4 + 4 = 8,' the girl answered TOCCLERRY. (9)
10. The father talked PIHAPLY about his new baby. (7)
11. The children answered the questions ASLYIE. (6)
12. The librarian whispered TELIQUY. (7)
13. The witch chanted her spells CLEDKWIY. (8)
14. The clown talked really FLYNUNI. (7)

Read the sentences and unjumble the anagrams to find the missing words. Write the word in the boxes under the anagram and on the line. Some letters have been written in for you.

 'Somebody has cheated,' the teacher

said _____ .

S	E	S	I	O	R	U	L	Y
S			I					

 The actress spoke her lines

_____ .

B	U	F	I	T	L	E	A	L	U	Y
B		U					L			

 The winner called out his number

_____ .

E	L	Y	D	X	I	T	E	C
E		C						

C	L	T	I	M	I	D	L	Y	Y	Q	Z	G
K	N	E	R	V	O	U	S	L	Y	W	M	M
M	J	H	E	A	S	I	L	Y	Y	I	T	F
T	F	G	A	W	X	U	K	L	R	C	R	H
C	F	O	R	P	F	N	L	Y	M	K	Z	K
O	K	W	O	R	P	U	X	L	J	E	N	F
R	M	F	E	L	F	I	Y	K	Y	D	Y	E
R	T	E	U	E	I	L	L	L	N	L	N	A
E	H	L	R	N	I	S	T	Y	I	Y	Z	G
C	T	A	W	R	N	E	H	S	W	V	K	E
T	C	N	G	Q	I	I	I	L	V	F	T	R
L	M	N	W	U	G	O	L	L	Y	H	Z	L
Y	A	T	Q	C	N	M	P	Y	F	W	M	Y

Word bank

CHEERFULLY	WICKEDLY	TIMIDLY	HAPPILY
NERVOUSLY	CAREFULLY	FUNNILY	QUIETLY
CORRECTLY	FOOLISHLY	EASYILY	ANGRILY
	EAGERLY	NOISILY	

35

Double consonant with ED and ING

When **ED** is added to a word (to make the past tense) or **ING** is added (to show the action is continuous), the final consonant is doubled, for example, *shop – sho**pp**ed/sho**pp**ing* and *grab – gra**bb**ed/gra**bb**ing*. The last letter isn't doubled when verbs end in **ER**, for example, *batter – battering*, or when verbs with two syllables end in **EN**, for example, *happen – happened/happening*. Some words can have the suffix **ING** but do not take **ED** to make the past tense, for example, *run – running*, but <u>not</u> *runned*.

Write the missing words in this table.

Root word	With suffix ED	With suffix ING
		chatting
skip		
	hopped	
		clapping
pin		
	dragged	

Change these sentences into the past tense. Write your new sentences on the lines. If the verb ends in **S**, you must remove it before adding **ED**, for example, *She **strums** her guitar – Yesterday she **strummed** her guitar.*

1. I **zip** up my jacket when I am cold. _____

2. He is angry and he **slams** the door. _____

3. She is tired and **flops** onto the bed. _____

4. He is upset and **quarrels** with his dad. _____

Put these words together into their family groups of three by crossing out the ones that are spelt wrongly and don't belong. One set has been done for you.

⭐1 drop   dropped   ~~droping~~   dropping   ~~droped~~

⭐2 run   ran   runing   running   runned

⭐3 swim   swam   swimming   swimmed   swimed   swiming

⭐4 drip   dripped   dripping   driped   drup

⭐5 flap   flapped   flaping   flapping

Double consonant with ER

These words all have the suffix **ER**. When **ER** is added to a root word, the final consonant is doubled for example, *big – bi**gg**er*. **ER** is sometimes used to make comparisons, for example, *fatter – thinner*. **ER** can also be used to describe a person who does something, for example, *She likes to **run** so she is a **runner***. The last letter usually isn't doubled when verbs with two syllables end in **N**, for example, *I will **open** the bottle with the bottle **opener***. An exception to this rule is *begin – beginner*.

Word bank

BATTER
BIGGER
DIGGER
DIMMER
FATTER
RUNNER
WETTER
WINNER
CHOPPER
DRUMMER
SHOPPER
SKIPPER
SLIMMER
SWIMMER
THINNER
BEGINNER

ACROSS

4. Another name for the captain of a ship or someone jumping with a rope (7)
6. Slimmer (7)
9. A person who has just started doing something, a novice (8)
11. Another name for an axe or a helicopter (7)
12. An antonym for loser (6)
13. This person exercises in water (7)
15. An antonym for thinner (6)
16. This machine can make big holes in the ground (6)

DOWN

1. This person hits the ball and scores runs (6)
2. An antonym for brighter (6)
3. The band member who keeps the beat (7)
5. A jogger or sprinter (6)
7. An antonym for smaller (6)
8. Someone who buys things (7)
10. A person who is on a diet and trying to lose weight (7)
14. Drier (6)

Hard and soft C

These words all contain the phoneme **C**, which can sound hard as in *cold* or soft as in *cell*. It is soft when followed by **E**, **I** or **Y**, for example, *cellar, pace, cinder, city* and *cycle*. It is hard when followed by any other vowel, for example, *cap, collar,* and *curve*, or any other letter (including another **C**), for example, *occur, neck, cloud, crisp* and *act*. It is also hard when found on its own at the end of words with more than one syllable, for example, *panic, rhythmic, electric, sonic, zodiac* and *maniac*.

Word bank

VICTOR	CLAP	TRACE	CLAIRE
CYLINDER	CENT	CONE	CROAK
CLEVER	CUT	SCAR	CLASS
CROOK	DICE	COLDER	FACE
CENTRE	CAT	CRACK	CREASE
RACE	ACE	COCOA	CRUEL
CELERY	CELL	CLOCKS	CEASE
CERTAIN	NICE	COT	CAKES
CELEBRATE	RICE	LACE	

ACROSS

1. A three-dimensional shape like a tube (8)
6. A line made by folding or crumpling (6)
7. A contest of speed (4)
8. Powdered seeds used to make chocolate (5)
9. A wound made by something sharp (3)
12. A girl's name (6)
13. A salad vegetable with a long juicy stalk (6)
15. The front of the head with features (4)
16. These are used to tell the time (6)
18. The middle or core (6)
20. The mark left by a healed wound (4)
22. The winner or conqueror (6)
26. To have festivities to mark a special day or occasion (9)
28. The noise of a frog (5)
29. A feline animal (3)
30. To stop or bring to an end (5)

DOWN

1. Definitely, for sure 'I am _ _ _ _ _ _ _' (7)
2. A delicate fabric usually white (4)
3. Small cubes with dots on used in board games (4)
4. White cereal eaten with curry (4)
5. To strike hands together and applaud (4)
6. A small room in a prison (4)
9. Hotter (antonym) (6)
10. A group of school pupils (5)
11. To make an exact copy through thin paper (5)
14. These are baked and can be fruit, sponge and so on (5)
16. Hand-held ice cream container (4)
17. Intelligent or skilful (6)
18. To split apart with a loud noise (5)
19. To be unkind or causing pain or suffering (5)
21. A shepherd's hooked staff, or a criminal (5)
23. A baby's bed (3)
24. Pleasant, friendly or kind (4)
25. A unit of money, one-hundredth of a dollar (4)
27. The number one playing card (3)

Hard and soft G

These words all contain the phoneme **G** which can be hard as in *gold* or soft as in *age*. It is usually soft when followed by **E**, **I** or **Y**, for example, *general*, *giraffe* and *gypsy*. It is also soft when it is in the letter string **DGE**, for example, *badge* and *dodger*. It is hard when followed by any other letter, for example, *gap*, *segment* and *juggle*. The hard **G** is usually found at the end of words, for example, *bag*, but not when words end in **ING**. The soft **G** phoneme is not as common at the beginning of words, but is usually found in the middle of words, for example, *page*, *energy* and *magic*.

Word bank

GULL	GARDEN	GROWL
GREEDY	GROUP	PEGS
GOOSE	RAGE	ORANGE
GARAGE	GREEN	GREY
EGG	GENIUS	FLAG
FINGER	GLAD	GOT
ENGINE	GUST	AGREE
GRUDGE	GAS	GAME
GHOSTS	GAG	FROG
ANGEL	WIG	GROAN

ACROSS

1. You can wear a ring on this (6)   **4.** Something you can play for fun or in competition (4)
5. A fairylike creature with wings and a halo (5)   **6.** You may feel angry if you bear a _ _ _ _ _ _ (6)
8. An angry dog may do this (5)   **12.** A place to grow plants (6)   **13.** To say 'yes', or to have the same opinion (5)   **14.** A number of people or objects together (5)   **15.** A web-footed water bird (5)   **16.** An airlike substance, helium is one type (3)   **18.** The past tense for get (3)   **19.** A sudden blast of wind (4)   **20.** An edible citrus fruit (6)   **22.** Another word for a motor (6)
24. The colour of white and black mixed together (4)

DOWN

1. A tadpole grows into this (4)   **2.** A synonym for happy (4)   **3.** Another word for violent anger (4)
4. A long-winged and web-footed sea bird (4)   **7.** You might find a car in here (6)   **8.** A very clever person with lots of ability (6)   **9.** False hair for the head (3)   **10.** These are used to hang up washing (4)   **11.** A banner that flies from a pole (4)   **12.** A synonym for spooks and spectres (6)   **15.** A low, deep sound of pain or sadness (5)   **17.** Always wanting more food or money (6)
19. The colour of grass (5)   **21.** This can be eaten scrambled or boiled (3)   **23.** A joke or a piece of cloth to stop someone speaking (3)

Words with OUGH

These words all contain the letter string **OUGH** but they are not all pronounced the same way. **OUGH** can be pronounced in many different ways. **OUGH** can sound like **UFF** as in *rough*, **OFF** as in *cough*, **OW** as in *bough*, **UH** as in *thorough* and **OO** as in *through*. **OUGH** can be followed by a **T** and this letter string also sounds different depending on the word, for example, *drought* and *nought*.

Sort these words into rhyming groups in the table below.

tough   trough   plough   drought   through   thorough   nought   brought   sought   enough

ROUGH	COUGH	BOUGH	BOUGHT	ODD ONES

Sort these words into word types in the table below. If words belong in more than one group, write them in each group, for example, *I have a **cough*** (noun) *and I **cough*** (verb) *all day*. If you are not sure of their meanings, check in a dictionary.

rough   enough   thoroughly   trough   plough   drought   ploughing   thorough
nought   bought   tough   brought   cough   sought   coughing   roughly   toughly   bough

Verb	Noun	Adjective	Adverb

Using the word bank to help you, put these missing **OUGH** words in these sentences.

Word bank
thorough
bought   trough
roughly   drought
ploughed

1. The farmer __ __ __ __ __ __ __ __ his fields and planted the corn.

2. I __ __ __ __ __ __ lots of food at the supermarket.

3. The pigs ate their food out of a __ __ __ __ __ __.

4. We had no rain for months and there was a __ __ __ __ __ __ __.

5. The little boy played with his toys very __ __ __ __ __ __ __ and broke them all.

6. The doctor did a very __ __ __ __ __ __ __ __ examination to find out what was wrong.

40

Words with OO

These words all contain the phoneme **OO**. The **OO** phoneme can be long, for example, *fool* and *room*, or it can be short, for example, *cook* and *foot*. It can also be spelt with a **U**, for example, *blue*, *fruit* and *lute*. **OO** can also be pronounced differently depending on dialect.

Sort these words into two groups in the table below.

boot stood good scooter toot neighbourhood cook
tool understood toadstool brook shoot wood book
food mood hoot look took loot

Long OO phoneme as in MOON		Short OO phoneme as in BOOK	

Put these words into rhyming groups in the table below, for example, *wood* rhymes with *good*.

bloom good toot cook tool brook shoot wood food
hoot look took loot pool fool cool proof hoof gloom
soon hoop droop brood room hood

BOOT	STOOD	SCOOT	BROOM	STOOL

BOOK	MOOD	ROOF	LOOP	NOON

Words with OW

Many words contain **OW** but they do not all sound the same, for example, listen to the difference between, *cow* and *show*.

Put the missing words into these sentences. On a separate piece of paper, sort the words into two groups according to their 'OW sound': **OW** as in CLOWN and '**OW** as in GROWN'.

| pillow | growling | bow | now | cows | owl |
| know | yellow | window | tomorrow | | |

1. At night I can hear the __ __ __ hooting.

2. The day after today is __ __ __ __ __ __ __ __.

3. Everyone had to __ __ __ down before the king.

4. I like a soft __ __ __ __ __ __ to put my head on at night.

5. 'Do it __ __ __!' instructed the teacher.

6. The guard dog was __ __ __ __ __ __ __ __ savagely at the burglar.

7. I closed the __ __ __ __ __ __ because the curtains were getting wet.

8. The farmer milks the __ __ __ __ every morning.

9. 'I __ __ __ __ the answer,' the student called out.

10. The daffodils were __ __ __ __ __ __ and white.

Find and circle or highlight the words from the word bank in the wordsearch.

Word bank

CROW	THROW
MOWER	LOWER
GROWN	BLOWN
SLOW	MOW
DROWN	TOW
SHOWER	SLOWER
TOWEL	TROWEL
GROW	FROWN
BROWN	FLOWER
POWER	TOWER
SNOW	CLOWN
CROWN	

T	T	O	W	E	L	R	B	L	O	W	N
C	H	G	J	N	S	L	M	O	W	R	R
R	X	R	W	W	F	H	C	T	E	M	L
O	Y	O	O	N	K	R	O	W	R	O	F
W	L	N	D	W	B	N	O	W	C	W	L
C	S	R	D	R	R	L	L	W	E	E	O
Y	L	M	D	P	O	E	L	N	N	R	W
T	O	W	E	R	W	W	W	G	R	W	E
J	W	Q	T	O	N	O	N	E	R	Q	R
T	E	C	R	T	R	T	W	N	F	O	P
O	R	T	Q	G	M	O	S	L	O	W	W
W	P	M	Y	L	P	G	C	R	O	W	N

Words with IND

These words all contain the letter string **IND** but they do not all have the same vowel phoneme. Some have a long **I** phoneme, for example, *find* and *kind*, but some have a short **I** phoneme, for example, *window* and *cinders*. Occasionally, some words can be spelt the same way but have different phonemes according to their meaning, for example, *The weather was very **windy** and the narrow road was **windy**.*

Put the missing words into these sentences.

 mind   find   hinder   binder   windows
cinders   blinds   kind   tinder   wind

1. The strong __ __ __ __ blew over lots of trees.

2. I put all the magazines for the year in a __ __ __ __ __ __ to keep them in order.

3. I cleaned the __ __ __ __ __ __ __ until the glass was sparkling.

4. A nosy person may be told to __ __ __ __ their own business.

5. The grate was full of ash and __ __ __ __ __ __ __ after the fire.

6. I pulled the __ __ __ __ __ __ to stop the sun coming in the window.

7. 'Are you going to help or __ __ __ __ __ __ me?' asked my mum.

8. To start a fire you need __ __ __ __ __ __ and dry wood.

9. We searched everywhere but couldn't __ __ __ __ the missing books.

10. The nurse was very __ __ __ __ and looked after me really well.

Sort the words into two groups in the table according to their **I** phoneme.

IND as in KIND	IND as in WINDOWS

Words with EA

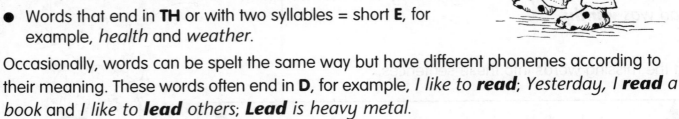

These words all contain the letter string **EA** but they do not all have the same vowel phoneme. Some have a long **E** phoneme, for example, *seat* and *dear*, but some have a short **E** phoneme, for example, *dead* and *heaven*. Here are some guidelines to help you:

- Words that end **E**, **CH**, **L**, **M**, **R** and **T** = long **E**, for example, *ease*, *reach*, *real*, *team*, *fear* and *meat*.
- Words that end in **TH** or with two syllables = short **E**, for example, *health* and *weather*.

Occasionally, words can be spelt the same way but have different phonemes according to their meaning. These words often end in **D**, for example, *I like to **read***; *Yesterday, I **read** a book* and *I like to **lead** others*; ***Lead** is heavy metal*.

Put the missing words into these sentences.

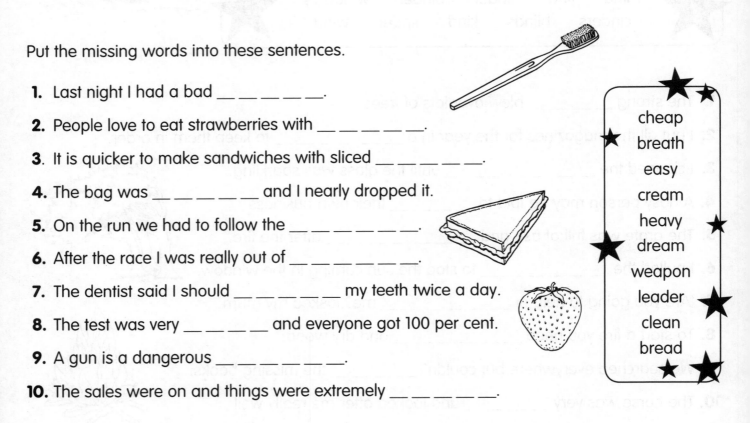

1. Last night I had a bad __ __ __ __ __.

2. People love to eat strawberries with __ __ __ __ __.

3. It is quicker to make sandwiches with sliced __ __ __ __ __ __.

4. The bag was __ __ __ __ __ and I nearly dropped it.

5. On the run we had to follow the __ __ __ __ __ __.

6. After the race I was really out of __ __ __ __ __ __.

7. The dentist said I should __ __ __ __ __ my teeth twice a day.

8. The test was very __ __ __ __ and everyone got 100 per cent.

9. A gun is a dangerous __ __ __ __ __ __.

10. The sales were on and things were extremely __ __ __ __ __.

cheap
breath
easy
cream
heavy
dream
weapon
leader
clean
bread

Sort the words into two groups in the table according to their vowel phoneme.

EA as in SEAT	EA as in HEAD

44

Words with EA

Put these words into the word ladders so that the last letter of one word is the first letter of the next. Some letters have been put in to help you.

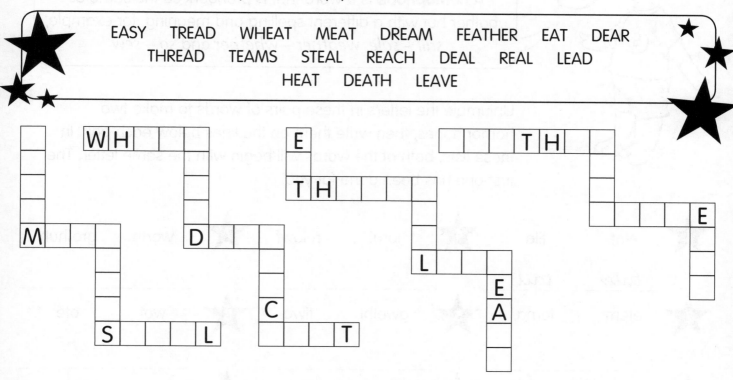

EASY   TREAD   WHEAT   MEAT   DREAM   FEATHER   EAT   DEAR
THREAD   TEAMS   STEAL   REACH   DEAL   REAL   LEAD
HEAT   DEATH   LEAVE

Put these words into rhyming groups in the table below, for example, *feat* rhymes with *heat*.

peach   tread   heather   thread   cheat   rear   heal   reach   peas
spread   treasure   seam   teach   heat   fear   steal   meal
scream   feather   head   team   fleas   measure   leather   dead
near   meat   clear   death   tease   each   wheat   stealthy
dear   stream   dream   heave   weave   real   wealthy

SEAT	YEAR	DEAL	HEALTHY	CREAM	LEAVE

BEACH	PLEASE	BREATH	BREAD	WEATHER	PLEASURE

Homophones

A **homophone** is a word that is pronounced the same as another but with a different spelling and meaning, for example, *sail – sale, weather – whether* and *so – sew.*

Unjumble the letters in these pairs of words to make two homophones, then write them on the lines below each pair. In these lists, both of the words will begin with the same letter. The first one has been done for you.

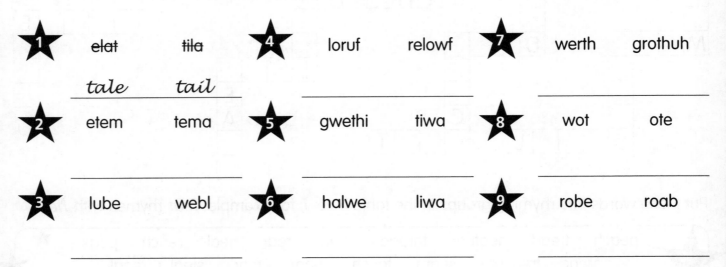

⭐1 elat   tila   ⭐4 loruf   relowf   ⭐7 werth   grothuh

      tale   *tail*   _____   _____

⭐2 etem   tema   ⭐5 gwethi   tiwa   ⭐8 wot   ote

_____   _____   _____

⭐3 lube   webl   ⭐6 halwe   liwa   ⭐9 robe   roab

_____   _____   _____

Fill in the correct homophones in these sentences.

1. When I _____ I always try to use the _____words. (**right, write**)

2. I used a drill and _____ a hole in the _____. (**board, bored**)

3. Under the _____ tree was a bear with brown _____. (**fir, fur**)

4. I went to town _____ bus to _____ some presents. (**buy, by**)

5. I had a _____ time at the circus. (**great, grate**)

6. It started to _____ as soon as I left the house. (**reign, rain**)

7. The children were _____; they did nothing all day. (**idol, idle**)

8. The line wasn't _____; I needed a ruler. (**strait, straight**)

9. The picture wasn't _____; it was fake. (**reel, real**)

10. On the _____ there were lots of different stalls. (**pier, peer**)

Homophones

Cross out the wrong word in the sentences below and circle the correct homophone in the wordsearch. One has been done for you.

1. During the flood, the water was **high/hi**.
2. I couldn't choose **witch/which** book to buy.
3. When I crossed the road, I tripped over the **kerb/curb**.
4. I couldn't decide what to **wear/where** to the party.
5. Come **hear/here** called the referee.
6. The **son/sun** was shining and I was so hot.
7. There was a high **tied/tide** and the waves crashed on the beach.
8. If you are dishonest, people may call you a **liar/lyre**.
9. Grapes can be crushed and made into **wine/whine**.
10. We lost the game **four/for** nil.
11. My teacher **reeds/reads** to us every day.
12. I buckled the belt around my **waist/waste**.
13. It was so horrible, I couldn't **bare/bear** it.
14. The **see/sea** was really rough.
15. The **bee/be** landed on the flower.

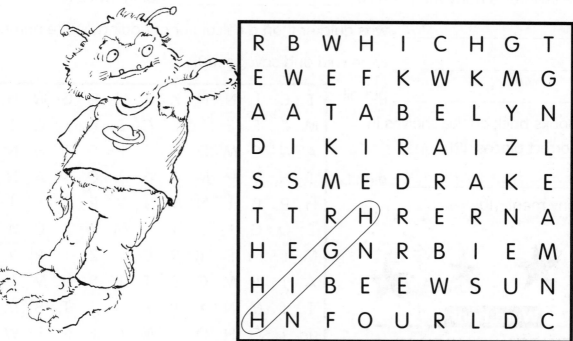

R	B	W	H	I	C	H	G	T
E	W	E	F	K	W	K	M	G
A	A	T	A	B	E	L	Y	N
D	I	K	I	R	A	I	Z	L
S	S	M	E	D	R	A	K	E
T	T	R	H	R	E	R	N	A
H	E	G	N	R	B	I	E	M
H	I	B	E	E	W	S	U	N
H	N	F	O	U	R	L	D	C

On a separate piece of paper, write your own sentences for the wrong words in the sentences above. Can you put more than one homophone in each sentence? For example, *The author wrote a funny **tale** about a dog that couldn't wag its **tail***.

Words with the suffixes IAN and CIAN

The suffixes **IAN** and **CIAN** mean 'of' or 'having to do with'. When added, they often describe a person, for example, a *historian*. **CIAN** is found at the end of words which originally ended in **C**, for example, *music – musician*. **IAN** (without the **C**) is added to words ending in other letters, for example, *Bulgaria – Bulgarian*. This usually happens when the root word ends in a **Y** (which changes to **I** to make **IAN**), for example, *Hungary – Hungarian*.

Using the word bank, complete the sentences and then circle or highlight the words in the wordsearch.

1. The talented _____ played a wide range of instruments. (8)

2. The _____ sorted out all the wiring in my house. (11)

3. I called a computer _____ when my laptop broke down. (10)

4. The ambitious _____ wanted to be prime minister. (10)

5. Her eyes were aching so she went to see an _____. (8)

6. At the children's party there was a _____ doing tricks. (8)

7. The _____ was quicker than a calculator at adding up the numbers. (13)

8. The _____ were wild and savage. (10)

9. The _____ put all the books back on the shelves in the correct places. (9)

10. The _____ didn't eat any meat. (10)

Word bank

MATHEMATICIAN	MUSICIAN
MAGICIAN	ELECTRICIAN
BARBARIANS	TECHNICIAN
LIBRARIAN	POLITICIAN
VEGETARIAN	OPTICIAN

T	C	L	N	N	K	J	H	R	G	W	H	C	C
M	E	F	E	L	E	C	T	R	I	C	I	A	N
A	N	C	M	D	H	P	L	P	T	N	N	R	N
T	H	V	H	M	A	G	I	C	I	A	N	A	M
H	P	B	L	N	M	J	Y	R	I	L	I	B	N
E	O	G	L	G	I	K	M	C	L	C	W	A	K
M	L	M	R	I	R	C	I	Z	I	R	Y	R	L
A	I	F	M	G	B	T	I	S	V	M	L	B	T
T	T	M	N	X	P	R	U	A	T	B	M	A	K
I	I	G	H	O	J	M	A	L	N	L	W	R	T
C	C	P	F	L	Z	T	R	R	J	R	H	I	Y
I	I	D	F	P	M	M	Z	M	I	Z	B	A	F
A	A	N	C	T	H	D	X	Z	L	A	K	N	D
N	N	V	E	G	E	T	A	R	I	A	N	S	B

Words with the prefixes IN, IM, IL and IR

The words in these puzzles have the prefixes **IL**, **IM**, **IN** or **IR**. These prefixes give the root word the opposite meaning, for example, *legal – illegal, personal – impersonal* and *complete – incomplete.* The following guidelines will help you:

- Words that begin with **L**, add the prefix **IL**, for example, *legible – illegible,* for **M** words add **IM**, for example, *mature – immature.*
- **N** words add **IN**, for example, *numerable – innumerable.*
- **R** words add **IR**, for example, *regular – irregular.*
- Words that begin with **P** or **B**, use **IM**, for example, *polite – impolite.*
- Words that begin with other letters (apart from **L** and **R**) add **IN**, for example, *accurate – inaccurate.*

Add either **IL**, **IM** or **IN** as a prefix to these words. Write the new word and say what it means, for example, *logical – illogical,* meaning absurd or meaningless and not logical.

1. legal – _____ means _____.

2. literate – _____ means _____.

3. possible – _____ means _____.

4. mature – _____ means _____.

5. credible – _____ means _____.

6. secure – _____ means _____.

Join the words to their correct prefixes and write the new words on a separate piece of paper. One has been done for you.

illegible → **IL**

IM

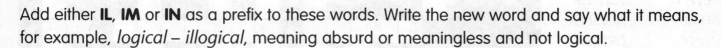

| legible | precise | legal | practical | complete | patient | sensitive |
| rational | capable | replaceable | audible | regular | pure | considerate |

IR

IN

49

Antonyms

An **antonym** is a word that has the opposite meaning (or nearly the opposite meaning) as another word. Antonyms can be adjectives, for example, *deep – shallow*, adverbs, for example, *loudly – quietly*, verbs, for example, *answered – asked*, or sometimes nouns, for example, *boy – girl*. Often adding or removing a prefix will also make an antonym, for example, *happy – unhappy*, *polite – impolite* and *disappear – a*.

You will find each type of antonym in this crossword. Read the clues and find, using the word bank to help you, the antonyms for the words in capital letters to get your answers.

Word bank

TO	BATTED
FAR	BOUGHT
MAN	FINISH
WET	SLOWLY
COOL	UNTIDY
EVEN	WINNER
FULL	AGAINST
TINY	DRESSED
LIGHT	ENEMIES
SHARP	HEAVILY
STALE	TIGHTLY
STAND	BELIEVED
UNDER	DISPLEASED
WORST	IMPOSSIBLE
YOUNG	

ACROSS

3. My water bottle was EMPTY (4)   **5.** The knife was BLUNT (5)   **7.** The paint was a DARK colour (5)   **9.** My dad says that nothing is POSSIBLE (10)   **14.** The man was OLD (5)   **16.** We are old FRIENDS (7)   **17.** Here is a letter FROM my friend (2)   **18.** The team won the toss and BOWLED (6)   **21.** I was tired at the START of the race (6)   **22.** I really felt like a LOSER (6)   **23.** I am going to SIT to watch the match (5)   **24.** I got UNDRESSED at the pool (7)   **25.** The spider was HUGE (4)   **26.** The clothes were DRY (3)   **27.** The athlete ran QUICKLY (6)

DOWN

1. The judge DISBELIEVED what the man said (8)   **2.** The bus stop wasn't that CLOSE (3)   **4.** My school desk is always NEAT (6)   **5.** The bread was FRESH (5)   **6.** The breeze was WARM (4)   **8.** My teacher was PLEASED with me (10)   **10.** It was an ODD number (4)   **11.** I am going to play FOR the red team (7)   **12.** The cargo ship was LIGHTLY loaded (7)   **13.** The jeweller SOLD a ring (6)   **15.** I am going OVER the bridge (5)   **19.** I tied my shoelaces LOOSELY (7)   **20.** I saw an elderly WOMAN (3)   **22.** The BEST thing about school is meeting my friends (5)

I before E except after C

When **E** and **I** are placed next to each other in a word with a long **E** phoneme, the **I** comes before the **E**, for example, *belief* and *field*. However, if these letters come after the letter **C** then they are written **EI**, for example, *conceit*, *receive* and *ceiling*. If there is no long **E** phoneme then the letters are also written **EI**, for example, *weight* and *reins*. Words such as *friend* and *caffeine* are exceptions as they do not fit the rule.

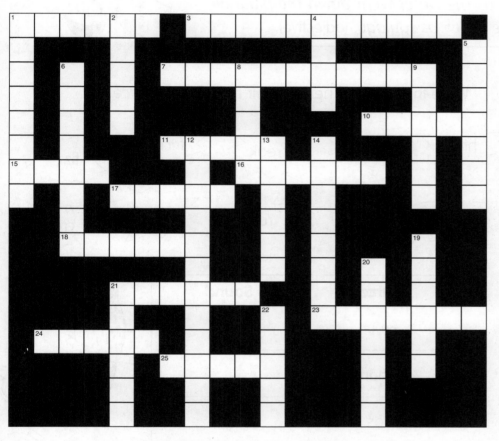

Word bank

CEILINGS	SHIELD
VEIN	GRIEF
CHIEF	NIECE
REVIEW	PERCEIVE
DECEIVE	FRIEZE
FIEND	PRIEST
SEIZE	RECEIPT
SHEIK	ACHIEVEMENT
THIEF	FRIEND
VIEW	SHRIEK
PIECE	RELIEVED
FIELDS	HANDKERCHIEF
RECEIVE	MISCHIEVOUS
FIERCE	

ACROSS

1. An official minister of a religion (6)
3. An accomplishment (11)
7. Naughty or playful (11)
10. To grab or grasp (5)
11. Someone who steals (5)
15. A blood vessel that takes blood to the heart (4)
16. A companion, buddy or mate (exception to the rule) (6)
17. A devilish, nasty person (5)
18. A piercing cry (6)
21. Savage and wild (6)
23. To betray, cheat or mislead (7)
24. Deep sadness or sorrow (5)
25. A bit or part of something (5)

DOWN

1. To understand or gain awareness of something (8)
2. An Arab chief (5)
4. A scene or panorama seen with the eyes (4)
5. An antonym for give (7)
6. These are the opposite of floors (8)
8. The boss, ruler or a leader of a tribe (5)
9. A piece of armour carried for protection (6)
12. A small square of fabric for nose wiping (12)
13. An ornamental band on a wall (6)
14. To feel calm or relaxed after stress or pain (8)
19. To assess or criticise a book or film (6)
20. Written proof of money that has been paid (7)
21. Areas of farmland for grazing or crops (6)
22. A brother or sister's daughter (5)

Onomatopoeia

The word **onomatopoeia** has Greek origins and means 'to make a name'. Words with onomatopoeia are called onomatopoeic and they imitate the sounds they are describing and so provide clues to the source of the sounds, for example, *A burst balloon goes **pop*** and *The sausages **sizzle** in the pan*. They can be everyday sounds or the particular sounds of animals and machines. Words with onomatopoeia can be verbs, nouns or adjectives, for example, *I **splashed** the water.* (verb); *I heard a **gurgle** as the water went down the plughole.* (noun); and *The clay was **squidgy**.* (adjective).

Write these words next to their most likely source.

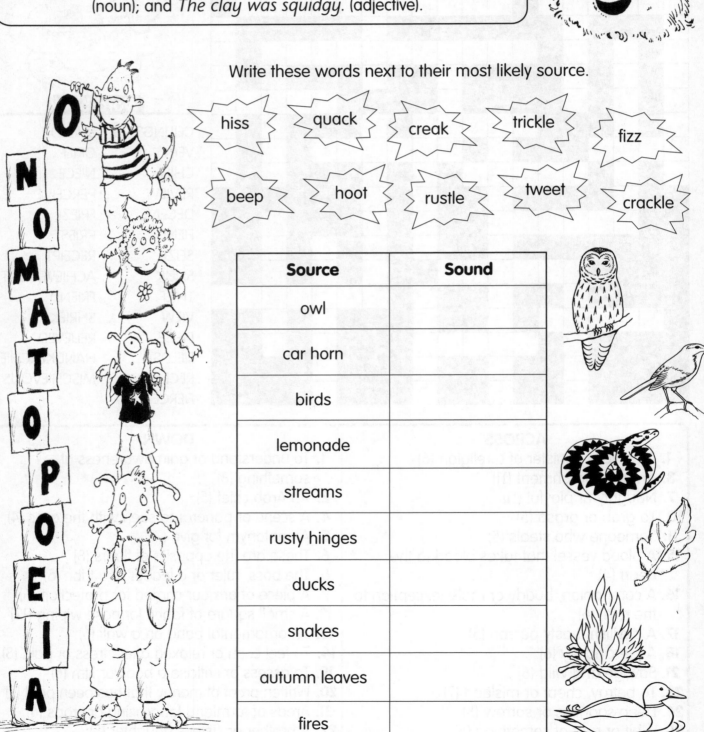

hiss   quack   creak   trickle   fizz

beep   hoot   rustle   tweet   crackle

Source	Sound
owl	
car horn	
birds	
lemonade	
streams	
rusty hinges	
ducks	
snakes	
autumn leaves	
fires	

Onomatopoeia

Using the word bank, find the onomatopoeic words in the wordsearch and write them in the sentences.

Word bank

SQUIRTING
GURGLED
ROAR
SQUEAL
WHACK
SCREECH
BANG
TINKLED
RUMBLE
WHOOSH
SQUEAKING
GIGGLING
CLANGED
HUM
SQUELCH

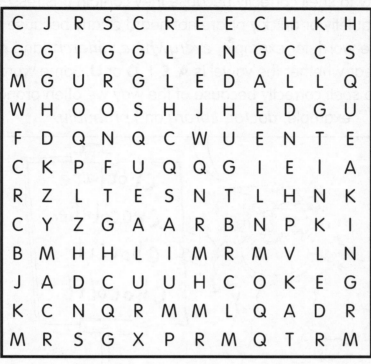

```
C J R S C R E E C H K H
G G I G G L I N G C C S
M G U R G L E D A L L Q
W H O O S H J H E D G U
F D Q N Q C W U E N T E
C K P F U Q Q G I E I A
R Z L T E S N T L H N K
C Y Z G A A R B N P K I
B M H H L I M R M V L N
J A D C U U H C O K E G
K C N Q R M M L Q A D R
M R S G X P R M Q T R M
```

1. My boots went _____ into the wet mud. (7)

2. The children began to _____ as the roller coaster went higher and higher. (6)

3. The mice were _____ in their cages. (9)

4. The firework went _____ up into the night sky. (6)

5. The little bell on the cat's collar _____ and warned the birds to fly away. (7)

6. We all heard the _____ of brakes as the car tried to stop. (7)

7. We didn't know the words but we could all _____ the tune. (3)

8. The _____ of thunder followed the flash of the lightning. (6)

9. When the team scored, the _____ of the crowd was deafening. (4)

10. The metal pipes _____ together when the man dropped them. (7)

11. The baby _____ happily when he saw his mum. (7)

12. The girls wouldn't stop _____ and their teacher was getting cross with them. (8)

13. We had great fun _____ each other with water. (9)

14. At the firework display, the rocket went _____ and made us jump. (4)

15. I heard the _____ of the cricket bat hitting the ball. (5)

Misspelt words with unstressed vowels

Some words are tricky to spell correctly because they contain unstressed vowels. These vowels are spoken quietly or quickly or are not heard clearly because the stress is on another syllable in the word, for example, *ev**e**rywhere*, *diff**e**rent* and ***a**round*. In these words it is hard to hear whether the vowel is **A**, **E**, **I**, **O** or **U**. Some words are also hard to remember how to spell correctly because of the way we often pronounce them, for example, *doctor*, *library* and *probably*.

choclate
chocolate
choclit
chocolit

Choose the correct spellings for these words with unstressed vowels and write them in the table.

	Choice of spellings				Correct spelling
1	CHOCLATE	CHOCOLATE	CHOCLIT	CHOCOLIT	
2	DIFFERENT	DIFFREENT	DIFFRUNT	DIFFERUNT	
3	RULA	RULER	RULOR	RULAH	
4	WEDNESDAY	WEDNSDAY	WENSDAY	WENDSDAY	
5	INTREST	INTEREST	INTRIST	INTOREST	
6	REGULY	REGULARLY	REGULALY	REGLY	
7	EVRYONE	EVREYONE	EVERRYONE	EVERYONE	
8	DEFINIT	DEFINATE	DEFINITE	DEFFNIT	
9	LIBRY	LIBERY	LIBARY	LIBRARY	
10	FEBRY	FEBUARY	FEBRUARY	FEBRARY	

Misspelt words with unstressed vowels

Circle or highlight the missing words in the wordsearch and write them in each sentence.

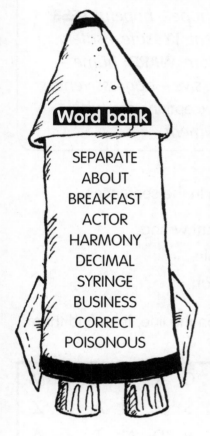

Word bank

SEPARATE
ABOUT
BREAKFAST
ACTOR
HARMONY
DECIMAL
SYRINGE
BUSINESS
CORRECT
POISONOUS

Y	H	A	R	M	O	N	Y	M	X	B
B	M	S	Y	R	I	N	G	E	S	J
U	C	T	D	B	W	T	F	U	M	B
S	O	W	P	E	U	X	O	D	E	R
I	R	V	Y	O	C	N	C	T	K	E
N	R	T	B	A	O	I	A	K	N	A
E	E	A	R	S	C	R	M	F	L	K
S	C	L	I	C	A	T	G	A	T	F
S	T	O	R	P	M	N	O	M	L	A
V	P	N	E	Q	P	C	J	R	K	S
T	G	S	L	C	L	L	F	T	M	T

1. I was reading a great book _____ motorbikes. (5)

2. The nurse used a _____ to inject medicine. (7)

3. When I grow up I want to be a famous _____ and win an Oscar. (5)

4. The _____ men were all wearing suits and ties. (8)

5. The snake was dangerous and its _____ venom could kill instantly. (9)

6. The choir all sang in perfect _____. (7)

7. When we do our maths we have to put the _____ point in the right place. (7)

8. 'Well done, that is the _____ answer,' said the teacher. (7)

9. In the morning, we all leapt out of bed and rushed down for _____. (9)

10. Our new house is much bigger and my sister and I have our own _____ bedrooms. (8)

Adding suffixes beginning with a consonant to words ending in E

There are a range of suffixes that can be added to words and different rules for applying them. The suffixes on this page begin with consonants and when they are added to words, the final **E** on the root word remains, for example, **FUL**: *hope – hopeful*; **LESS**: *care – careless*; **MENT**: *excite – excitement*; **LY**: *safe – safely*; **WISE**: *like – likewise*; **DOM**: *free – freedom*; **WARD**: *home – homeward*; **LIKE**: *life – lifelike*; **NESS**: *agressive – aggressiveness* and **WORTHY**: *praise – praiseworthy*. Exceptions are *wise – wisdom* and *argue – argument*.

Add the correct suffix (**LESS**, **FUL** or **LY**) to these words and write them in the sentences.

1. FATE: It was on that _____ day that everything went wrong.

2. TIRE: She was a _____ campaigner for poor people.

3. NICE: The little boy spoke very _____ to the librarian.

Add the correct suffix to the words in the word bank and write them on the line, then find them in the wordsearch.

Word bank

FATE _____

LIFE _____

HOME _____

LIKE _____

LONE _____

PRAISE _____

EXCITE _____

PAVE _____

LOVE _____

BRAVE _____

TIRE _____

CARE _____

LATE _____

AGE _____

HOPE _____

HATE _____

G	T	P	R	A	I	S	E	W	O	R	T	H	Y	M
P	P	L	A	T	E	N	E	S	S	Z	Q	A	C	Z
A	X	R	L	J	D	V	N	X	R	D	N	T	Z	A
V	M	M	I	P	C	M	M	P	H	Y	D	E	V	G
E	R	W	K	L	I	F	E	L	I	K	E	F	F	E
M	X	L	E	C	T	N	T	E	Q	S	T	U	T	L
E	N	C	W	T	J	H	M	I	S	P	K	L	U	E
N	J	N	I	R	L	O	O	E	R	Z	T	F	M	S
T	Q	K	S	T	S	H	L	M	G	E	E	Z	V	S
L	T	V	E	E	E	E	O	R	E	T	L	Y	M	M
J	N	L	N	K	R	M	M	P	A	W	L	E	D	T
R	K	O	W	A	H	K	E	F	E	E	A	D	S	R
F	L	V	C	L	R	W	Q	N	V	F	T	R	Y	S
B	R	A	V	E	L	Y	Q	O	T	D	U	G	D	L
D	M	D	H	R	K	Z	L	R	Q	M	C	L	Y	B

Adding the suffixes S, ED, ER, EST and ING to words ending in Y

When suffixes are added to words with a final **Y**, sometimes the **Y** remains and sometimes it changes to an **I**. Look at the rules below. If words have:

● a final **Y** (after a consonant) when **S**, **ED** and **ER** are added, the **Y** becomes an **I**, for example, *supply – supplies, supplied, supplier*;

● a final **Y** (after a vowel) when **S**, **ED** and **ER** are added, the **Y** remains, for example, *play – plays, played, player*;

● a final **Y** (after a consonant or a vowel) when **ING** is added, the **Y** always remains, for example, *play – playing*.

The answers to the crossword have the suffixes **S**, **ED**, **ER** or **ING** and the root words all end in **Y**.

Word bank

REPLIED	SATISFIED
RELYING	WORRIED
DEFIED	FRAYED
BUYING	DISPLAYED
ENJOYS	REPLAYED
STAYED	DESTROYED
BURIED	MAGNIFYING

ACROSS

1. My little brother _ _ _ _ _ _ watching cartoons (6)   **3.** The pictures were all _ _ _ _ _ _ _ _ _ in the art gallery (9)   **5.** The blanket was old and _ _ _ _ _ _ around the edges (6)   **6.** I was really _ _ _ _ _ _ _ about my friend who was sick (7)   **11.** The earthquake _ _ _ _ _ _ _ _ _ the town (9)   **12.** I _ _ _ _ _ _ _ to my friend's letter straight away (7)   **13.** Making something bigger (10)   **14.** They _ _ _ _ _ _ _ _ the goal on the TV lots of times (8)

DOWN

2. I would have liked to have _ _ _ _ _ _ longer, but I had to go (6)   **4.** An antonym for obeyed (6)   **7.** We were _ _ _ _ _ _ _ on our friend to bring a ball for the game (7)   **8.** Contented or fulfilled (9)   **9.** I enjoy _ _ _ _ _ _ new clothes in the sales (6)   **10.** My dog _ _ _ _ _ _ his bone in the garden (6)

Verbs and the past tense ED

Regular verbs follow these rules, when **ED** is added to make the past tense. If the verb ends in:

- **E**, just add **D**, for example, *wave – waved*;
- two consonants or a vowel before **Y**, add **ED**, for example, *knock – knocked*;
- a consonant and **Y**, change to **I** and add **ED**, for example, *hurry – hurried*;
- one consonant with a short vowel phoneme, double the consonant and add **ED**, for example, *shop – shopped*.

> The last letter isn't doubled when verbs end in **ER**, for example, *batter – battered*, or when verbs end in **N** and they have two syllables, for example, *happen – happened*.

Change the words in the word bank into past tense verbs with **ED** to make your answers to the crossword clues.

Word bank

RENT	PLAY	LAND
TIRE	ASK	HAPPEN
DAZE	RACE	JUMP
WAIT	LIE	DREAD
END	THREAD	OPEN
HOPE	WATCH	DRY
CHOP	PLEASE	EVOLVE
DANCE	PRETEND	
PUSH	DRILL	

ACROSS

1. Paid to use some land or a home (6)　**4.** Occurred or took place (8)　**6.** Took part in a contest of speed (5)　**8.** Happy or contented (7)　**9.** Removed water (5)　**11.** Stopped or finished (5)　**12.** Observed or looked at (7)　**14.** Arrived on the ground (6)　**15.** Waltzed or jived (6)　**18.** A synonym for questioned (5)　**20.** It means the same as wished or desired (5)　**21.** Feeling sleepy (5)　**22.** Leaped up or over something (6)　**23.** Made holes with a tool (7)　**24.** Faked or acted (9)

DOWN

2. A needle with cotton is _ _ _ _ _ _ _ _ (8)　**3.** Dizzy and bewildered (5)　**5.** An antonym for closed (exception to rule – don't double final consonant) (6)　**7.** Served food and drink in a restaurant (6)　**8.** An antonym for pulled (6)　**10.** Gradually changed (as in evolution) (7)　**13.** The opposite of worked (6)　**16.** Cut with sharp blows (7)　**17.** Greatly feared (7)　**19.** Didn't tell the truth (4)

Verbs with ING

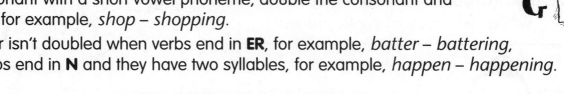

These verbs have **ING** endings which means that the action described by the verb is continuous, for example, *I am walking today. I was walk**ing** yesterday* and *I will be walk**ing** tomorrow*. The words in this puzzle are regular verbs that follow the rules below. If the verb ends in:

- **E**, take off the **E** and add **ING**;
- two consonants or a **Y** or **W**, add **ING**, for example, *knock – knocking*;
- one consonant with a short vowel phoneme, double the consonant and add **ING**, for example, *shop – shopping*.

The last letter isn't doubled when verbs end in **ER**, for example, *batter – battering*, or when verbs end in **N** and they have two syllables, for example, *happen – happening*.

Give the words in the word bank an **ING** ending to make your answers.

Word bank

CHANGE	WALK
ASK	LAUGH
COME	WATCH
KNOW	NUMBER
LEAVE	BAKE
LIGHT	YAWN
START	SING
STOP	PARK
SWIM	BUBBLE
TURN	RUN

ACROSS

2. Driving your car into a space and leaving it there (7)   **7.** Observing or looking at (8)
8. Strolling (7)   **10.** You will hear people in a choir doing this (7)   **11.** An antonym for going (6)
14. Putting a match to wood to make a fire (8)   **18.** Cooking cakes in the oven (6)   **19.** Writing numerical digits on things (9)

DOWN

1. You may be doing this if you are tired (7)   **3.** Jogging or sprinting (7)   **4.** Having information (7)   **5.** Giggling, chortling or guffawing (8)   **6.** An antonym for answering (6)   **9.** An antonym for staying (7)   **11.** Altering (8)   **12.** Fizzing with gas, like a glass of champagne or lemonade (8)
13. Ceasing (8)   **15.** An antonym for stopping (8)   **16.** Doing freestyle, backstroke or breaststroke (8)   **17.** Changing direction (7)

The prefixes PRO and SUS

PRO has Greek and Latin roots and can mean, 'in favour of', for example, *pro-active* or 'instead of', *pronoun*. However, in many words that begin with **PRO**, these meanings aren't obvious or don't seem to apply. **PRO** can be pronounced with a long **O** phoneme as in *profile*, or a short **O** as in *profit*. When **PRO** is used to mean 'in favour of' it is sometimes used with a hyphen, for example, *pro-war*.

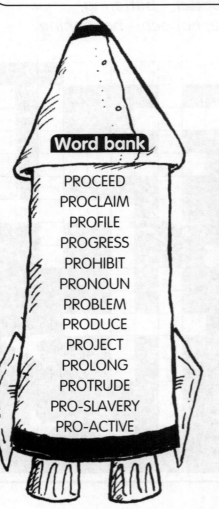

Word bank

PROCEED
PROCLAIM
PROFILE
PROGRESS
PROHIBIT
PRONOUN
PROBLEM
PRODUCE
PROJECT
PROLONG
PROTRUDE
PRO-SLAVERY
PRO-ACTIVE

Solve the clues and use the word bank to help you to complete this crossword.

ACROSS
1. To forbid or ban (8) **2.** A plan, scheme or task (7) **6.** A question or difficulty to be solved (7) **7.** A word that takes the place of a noun (7) **8.** To be positive and in favour of doing something (10 including a hypen) **9.** To announce publicly (8) **10.** If you work hard you will make _ _ _ _ _ _ _ _ (8)

DOWN
1. In favour of making people slaves (11 including a hypen) **3.** To make or create something (7) **4.** To go forward (7) **5.** To stick out (8) **7.** To lengthen (7) **8.** An outline of the face from the side (7)

The prefixes PRO and SUS

These words begin with the prefix **SUS** which comes from a Latin word meaning 'up'.
Unjumble the anagrams in brackets and put the missing words into the sentences.

1. The policeman said, 'You look guilty and I _____ you are to blame.' (CUSPSET)

2. Use of the pool was _____ until the water was clean. (DEDSPUNES)

3. My big brother loves thrillers full of _____ and action. (SENSUPES)

4. I saw some _____ characters and called the police. (USISPOCSIU)

5. I couldn't _____ my interest and I fell asleep. (SAINTUS)

6. Fair skinned people are _____ to sunburn. (SCIPUSEBELT)

Join these word chunks to their correct prefix and write them on the line below. One has been completed for you.

PRO

CESS	PECT	PEND	PERTY	VIDE	TAIN	DUCTION	PICION

SUS

PROCESS _____

_____

Words with the prefixes IN, IM, IL and IR revision

The answers to this crossword have the prefixes **IN**, **IM**, **IL** or **IR**. These prefixes make the root words have the opposite meaning, for example, *legal – illegal, personal – impersonal, complete – incomplete* and *responsible – irresponsible*. Sometimes they can mean 'in', 'into' or 'to make', for example, *illuminate, import* and *indoors*.

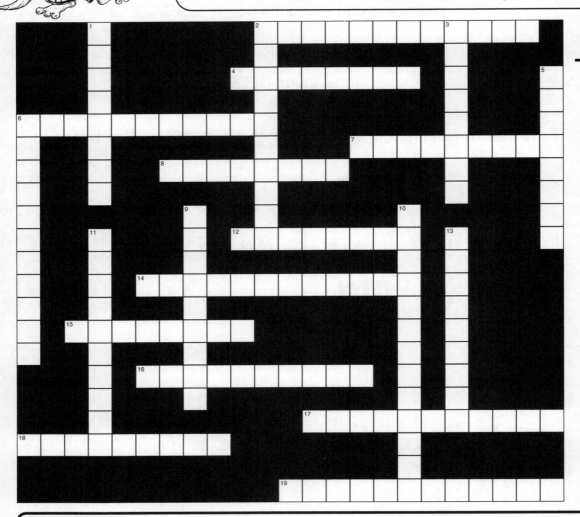

Word bank
IMMATERIAL
IMMATURE
IMPERFECT
INARTICULATE
INCOMPLETE
INCONVENIENT
INDEPENDENT
ILLUSION
IMMOBILE
IMMIGRANT
IMMORTAL
IMPARTIAL
IMPRACTICAL
IMPOVERISHED
INADEQUATE
INANIMATE
INCREASE
INDECENT
INDESCRIBABLE
INFERIOR
INTOLERABLE

ACROSS
2. Annoying and not suitable (12)   **4.** Childish (8)   **6.** Separate and unconnected (11)
7. Lifeless (9)   **8.** Substandard or poor quality (8)   **12.** A fantasy or hallucination (8)
14. Unable to express yourself clearly (12)   **15.** Able to live for ever (8)   **16.** Insufficient and not enough (10)   **17.** OK in theory but not sensible or feasible (11)   **18.** With faults and not flawless (9)   **19.** Poor and weak (12)

DOWN
1. To grow bigger or greater in number (8)   **2.** Unimportant and not relevant, for example, What you say is _ _ _ _ _ _ _ _ _ _ (10)   **3.** Still and unmoving (8)   **5.** Rude or offensive (8)
6. Unbearable (11)   **9.** Unbiased and fair (9)   **10.** Beyond description or explanation (13)
11. Unfinished (10)   **13.** A settler in a foreign country (9)

The suffixes ER and EST

Adjectives are words that describe a noun and add to its meaning. The suffixes **ER** and **EST** are added to make comparison. For example, *Julie is tall**er** than Carole, but Brian is the tall**est***. The rules for adding **ER** and **EST** are the same as for adding **ED**. For words with:

- a final **E**, just add **R** or **EST**, for example, *late – later/latest*;
- two final consonants or a long vowel phoneme, just add **ER** or **EST**, for example, *old – older/oldest*;
- a final **Y**, change the **Y** to **I** and add **ER** or **EST**, for example, *easy – easier/easiest*;
- one final consonant with a short vowel phoneme, double the consonant and add **ER** or **EST**, for example, *sad – sadder/saddest*.

Add **ER** or **EST** to the adjectives in the word bank and write them on the line, then find them in the wordsearch. Use the clues to help you.

Word bank

LIGHT _____

EARLY _____

QUICK _____

NOISY _____

EASY _____

LAZY _____

HAPPY _____

SLOW _____

CHEAP _____

SOFT _____

UGLY _____

HOT _____

WIDE _____

NICE _____

U	G	L	I	E	S	T	M	K	K	C	R
R	X	Q	X	J	T	W	T	Y	R	E	R
M	M	Y	U	C	M	S	P	E	C	E	V
T	L	A	Z	I	E	S	T	I	I	C	S
K	G	F	H	T	C	H	N	S	H	H	L
N	Q	W	F	A	G	K	A	L	L	E	O
O	H	O	I	I	P	E	E	Z	H	A	W
I	S	N	L	D	T	P	L	S	T	P	E
S	H	O	T	T	E	R	I	T	T	E	R
I	R	M	Q	N	Y	R	C	E	V	S	K
E	A	R	L	I	E	S	T	N	S	T	R
R	F	G	M	Y	K	H	N	R	G	T	C

1. An antonym for heavier (7)   **2.** A synonym for fastest (8)   **3.** An antonym for most expensive (8)   **4.** An antonym for faster (6)   **5.** An antonym for hardest (7)   **6.** An antonym for nastier (5)   **7.** An antonym for narrower (5)   **8.** An antonym for more difficult (6)   **9.** An antonym for most energetic and hard working (7)   **10.** A synonym for most joyful (8)   **11.** An antonym for prettiest (7)   **12.** An antonym for quieter (7)   **13.** An antonym for latest (8)   **14.** An antonym for colder (6)

The suffix ISH

The suffix **ISH** means 'having the quality of', for example, *childish*. **ISH** can also mean 'belonging to', for example, *British*, but sometimes the root word may have to be changed, for example, *Spain – Spanish*. **ISH** can be added directly to some words, for example, *baby – babyish*. However, when added to some words, the final consonant has to be doubled, for example, *fat – fattish*. When **ISH** is added to some words ending in **E**, the **E** is removed first, for example, *prude – prudish*. **ISH** can also be added to adjectives to indicate approximation, for example, *fairly tall – tallish*.

Write the root words for these words with the suffix **ISH**.

Root word	Word with ISH
	selfish
	childish
	British
	foolish
	loutish
	brutish
	hellish
	sluggish
	ticklish
	sheepish

Add **ISH** to these words to make informal words (meaning approximation) and put them in a sentence.

1. black – _____

2. small – _____

3. thin – _____

4. round – _____

The suffix ISM

The suffix **ISM** has Greek origins. It means 'a state of being', 'belief' or 'action'. Words that end in **ISM** are nouns, for example, *perfectionism* and *cannibalism*.

In the table below, write in the missing letters or definitions. The first one has been done for you.

Word	Definition
RACISM	The belief that your own race of people is better than others.
F __ __ __ __ ISM	The belief that women have the same rights as men.
CA __ __ __ __ __ __ ISM	The action of an animal that eats its own kind.
CR __ __ __ __ ISM	A comment or judgement about another person.
MAGNETISM	
HEROISM	
W __ __ __ ICISM	A funny or amusing remark.
VEGETARIANISM	
ATHEISM	
JOURNALISM	
VAN __ __ __ ISM	The act of deliberately breaking or spoiling things.

In the table below, write in the missing words. Put in as many words in the same family as you can think of.

Word with ISM	Words in the same family			
PERFECTIONISM	PERFECT	PERFECTIONIST	PERFECTLY	
AMERICANISM				
	ANARCHY	ANARCHIST	ANARCHIC	ANARCHICAL
ATHLETICISM				
ESCAPISM				
RACISM				
	MYSTICAL	MYSTIC		
MAGNETISM				
	HERO			
	VANDAL			

The suffix ION

The suffix **ION** changes verbs into nouns and means 'the act, state, result or process of'. **T**, **AT**, **S** or **SS** can be added to **ION** to make **TION**, **ATION**, **SION** or **SSION**, for example, *infection*, *exploration*, *television* and *procession*. These endings all sound similar (rather like **SHUN**). However, there is a subtle difference between their pronunciation. Say these three words aloud to hear the difference: *division*, *action* and *admission*.

In most examples when the suffixes are added, the root words also change a little. Look at the examples below for words with **TION** and complete the tables.

Root word (verb)	Changed root word	New word with suffix (noun)
DIRECT	Final **T** so just add **ION**	DIRECTION
PROTECT		
INVENT		

Root word (verb)	Changed root word	New word with suffix (noun)
ROTATE	Remove final **E** and add **ION**	ROTATION
SEPARATE		
EDUCATE		

Look at the examples below for words with **ATION** and complete the tables.

Root word (verb)	Changed root word	New word with suffix (noun)
EXAMINE	Remove final **E** and add **ATION**	EXAMINATION
EXPLORE		
STARVE		

Look at the examples below for words with **SION** and complete the tables.

Root word (verb)	Changed root word	New word with suffix (noun)
SUPERVISE	Remove final **E** and add **ION**	SUPERVISION
REVISE		
TELEVISE		

Root word (verb)	Changed root word	New word with suffix (noun)
EXPLODE	Remove final **DE** and add **SION**	EXPLOSION
CONCLUDE		
DIVIDE		

Join these words to their correct suffix and write them on a separate piece of paper. One has been completed for you.

TION   *DIVISION* ———→ **SION**

| DIVIDE | PROTECT | COLLECT | EXPLODE | ROTATE | COLLIDE | INVENT | CONFUSE |

The suffix ION

Change the verbs in the clues to nouns with the suffix **ION** to make your answers.

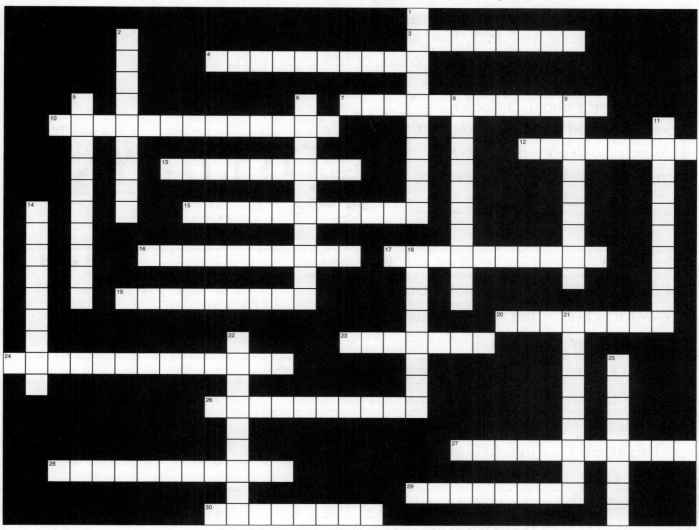

ACROSS

3. ELECT (8)
4. IMPRESS (10)
7. APPRECIATE (12)
10. DECOMPOSE (13)
12. CREATE (8)
13. COLLIDE (9)
15. SUBTRACT (11)
16. CONCLUDE (10)
17. IRRIGATE (10)

19. IMITATE (9)
20. INCISE (8)
23. ERODE (7)
24. CONTRADICT (13)
26. TELEVISE (10)
27. ASSOCIATE (11)
28. PROGRESS (11)
29. DIVISE (8)
30. INVADE (8)

DOWN

1. GENERATE (10)
2. EXPLODE (9)
5. RELAX (10)
6. MOTIVATE (10)
8. COLLECT (10)
9. OPERATE (9)
11. POPULATE (10)
14. OBJECT (9)
18. REVISE (8)
21. INVENT (9)
22. DIRECT (9)
25. ADD (8)

The suffix OLOGY

The suffix **OLOGY** or **LOGY** has Greek origins and basically means 'the study of', for example, *geology*. The suffix **OLOGIST** describes a person who studies that field, for example, *geologist*. Words such as *anthology* and *eulogy* are exceptions as they are not areas of study; in these words **OLOGY** means 'a type of speech or writing'.

These words and definitions have been muddled up. Write the correct word next to each definition and cross it off the list. The first one has been done for you.

Word	Definition	Correct word
CARDIOLOGY	The study of micro-organisms.	MICROBIOLOGY
DERMATOLOGY	The study of life and living organisms.	
CHRONOLOGY	The study of society.	
TOXICOLOGY	A collection of poems, songs or stories.	
HYDROLOGY	The scientific study of crime.	
BIOLOGY	The study animals.	
THEOLOGY	The study of the skull.	
ASTROLOGY	The study of the weather.	
BACTERIOLOGY	The study of bacteria.	
ECOLOGY	The study of the relationships between living organisms and their environment.	
METEOROLOGY	The study of the stars to foretell events.	
ZOOLOGY	The study of poisons.	
CRANIOLOGY	The study of things arranged in order of time or the study of time itself.	
ANTHOLOGY	The branch of medicine that deals with the skin.	
SOCIOLOGY	The study of god.	
CRIMINOLOGY	The study of water.	
~~MICROBIOLOGY~~	The study of the heart.	
PSYCHOLOGY	The study of the mind and mental processes in humans.	

The suffixes ISE and IFY

The suffixes **ISE** and **IFY** mean 'to make'. They can be added to words and usually change nouns into verbs, for example, *He was a **vandal*** (noun) and *he was going to **vandalise*** (verb) *the house* and *He was a **terror*** (noun) *and he used to **terrify*** (verb) *me*. However, sometimes they can also change adjectives into verbs, for example, *The Dr wanted to use **sterile*** (adjective) *instruments and asked the nurse to **sterilise*** (verb) *them*. **ISE** can be added directly to words ending in a consonant, for example, *verbal – verbalise*. When adding the suffix **IFY**, the root word has to be changed and often the last syllable or final vowel is removed before **IFY** is added, for example, *pure – purify*.

Complete the missing words in the sentences and then find them in the wordsearch. They all have the suffixes **ISE** or **IFY**.

1. We had to provide evidence to _____ our arguments. (7)

2. To go out and mix with people. (9) _____

3. To speak your thoughts or ideas out loud. (9) _____

4. To calm someone down and stop a fight. (6) _____

5. To worship someone and look up to them excessively. (7) _____

6. The students had to _____ their designs to make them work better. (6)

7. He had to _____ the mistakes the others had made and put them right. (7)

8. In the police line up, I was told to _____ the criminal. (8)

9. To strengthen, the soldiers had to _____ their defences. (7)

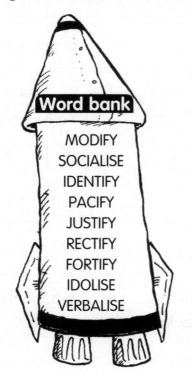

Word bank

MODIFY
SOCIALISE
IDENTIFY
PACIFY
JUSTIFY
RECTIFY
FORTIFY
IDOLISE
VERBALISE

P	G	M	F	R	I	R	N	Y	J	M	F
A	L	O	B	O	C	D	F	Z	Y	M	N
C	A	D	V	D	R	I	O	F	V	E	G
I	D	I	H	E	T	T	I	L	T	L	Y
F	M	F	K	N	R	T	I	I	I	F	T
Y	P	Y	E	M	S	B	L	F	I	S	N
Q	L	D	Y	U	Y	U	A	T	Y	Q	E
W	I	V	J	D	S	M	C	L	B	D	R
X	G	R	M	E	T	E	P	R	I	Y	Y
K	Y	V	D	L	R	K	B	F	F	S	G
F	S	O	C	I	A	L	I	S	E	R	E
T	L	A	N	Q	P	I	L	L	F	N	D

The suffix FUL

These words end in the suffix **FUL**. This suffix changes the root word into an adjective. For example, *I am so tired I need a **rest**, so I am going to have a **restful** weekend*. Sometimes adding the suffix **FUL** instead of the suffix **LESS** can make a word mean the opposite too, for example, *careless – careful* and *powerless – powerful*.

Two important things to remember:
1. The suffix **FUL** has one **L** at the end and not two, for example, – *restful* not *restfull*.
2. In words that end in a consonant and then **Y**, the **Y** changes to **I** when you add the suffix **FUL**, for example, *beauty – beautiful*.

These words have two syllables and they all end in **FUL**. Read the clues and write the answers. Use the anagrams in brackets to help you.

1. When I hit my friend by accident with the hockey stick I felt _____. (FLAUW)

2. I don't know if I am going to win, but I am really _____. (FLUPHOE)

3. A synonym for grateful. (KFULHATN)

4. A synonym for awful or terrible. (DDRAEFLU)

5. A toothbrush is really _____ for cleaning your teeth. (FUSEUL)

6. When my friend helped me clean my room I was so _____ I gave her a hug. (RATGELUF)

7. My friend is so _____ she is always smiling and laughing. (FLCEHERU)

8. Someone who thinks a lot is really _____. (UTHGFLUOHT)

9. My little kitten is so _____. (FALUPLY)

What is the mystery word spelt out in the grey boxes? It means amazing, remarkable or superb. Write a sentence for the mystery word on the line below.

The suffix FUL

In this crossword the answers all end in **FUL**. Add the **FUL** suffix to the words in the word bank and write them on the line to make your answers. Then complete the crossword.

Word bank

BEAUTY _____

SUCCESS _____

POWER _____

FORGET _____

FEAR _____

JOY _____

FRET _____

GLEE _____

PLENTY _____

WILL _____

PURPOSE _____

WATCH _____

ACROSS

1. An antonym for aimless or without direction (10)   **5.** _ _ _ _ _ _ _ children do not listen to others and just do what they want (7)   **8.** A synonym for strong and in charge (8)   **10.** Full of worry or anxiety (7)   **11.** Someone who is scared is _ _ _ _ _ _ _ (7)   **12.** An antonym for ugly (9)

DOWN

2. This type of person always does well or is a winner (10)   **3.** Always on the look out (8)
4. This means ecstatic or over the moon with happiness (7)   **6.** The food was _ _ _ _ _ _ _ _ _; there was lots to go round (9)   **7.** I am so _ _ _ _ _ _ _ _ _; I can never remember anything (9)
9. This means very happy (6)

The suffix EN

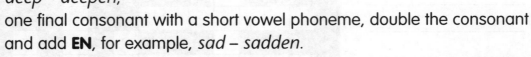

The suffix **EN** means 'to make', but is used less frequently. **EN** can be added to adjectives to make them into verbs, for example, *The potter was using **soft** clay.* (adjective) – *The potter was going to **soften** the clay.* (verb). **EN** can also be added to verbs, for example, *I **shake**. – I was badly **shaken** by what I saw.*

The rules for adding **EN** are like those for adding **ER**. If words have:
- a final **E**, just add **N**, for example, *wide – widen*;
- two final consonants or a long vowel phoneme, just add **EN**, for example, *deep – deepen*;
- one final consonant with a short vowel phoneme, double the consonant and add **EN**, for example, *sad – sadden*.

Write in the missing words in this table and write a short sentence for each. The first one has been done for you.

Root word	Verb with EN	Sentence
dark	darken	I had to darken the paint on the doors to match the walls.
	flatten	
haste		
	strengthen	
	cheapen	
tight		

Use the word bank to help you to solve the clues to complete the sentences and the mini-crossword.

Word bank

FLATTEN
WEAKEN
WIDEN
TIGHTEN

ACROSS
3. The council had plans to _ _ _ _ _ the narrow road. (5)
4. We are going to _ _ _ _ _ _ _ the land and build our house. (7)

DOWN
1. I had to _ _ _ _ _ _ _ my belt to stop my trousers falling down. (7)
2. The disease was beginning to _ _ _ _ _ _ the young and the elderly. (6)

Suffixes revision

Here are the suffixes that you will have met previously in your spelling work: **ABLE, AL, ARY, ATE, CIAN, ED, EN, ER, ESS, EST, ETTE, FUL, HOOD, IAN, IBLE, IC, IFY, ING, ISE, ISH, ISM, IST, LIKE, MENT, NESS, OLOGY, SHIP, SION, TION** and **WORTHY**.

★ ★

Decide which of the following suffixes belongs to each of the words (or parts of words) below and write the new words on the lines. Each suffix is only used once.

ABLE, AL, ARY, ATE, CIAN, ED, EN, ER, ESS, EST, ETTE, FUL, HOOD, IAN, IBLE.

★1 sense – _____

★2 strength – _____

★3 beauty – _____

★4 neighbour – _____

★5 prince – _____

★6 music – _____

★7 enjoy – _____

★8 jump – _____

★9 library – _____

★10 electric – _____

★11 loud – _____

★12 teach – _____

★13 second – _____

★14 decor – _____

★15 launder – _____

★ ★

Decide which of the following suffixes belongs to each of the words (or parts of words) below and write the new words on the lines. Each suffix is only used once.

IC, IFY, ING, ISE, ISH, ISM, IST, LIKE, MENT, NESS, OLOGY, SHIP, SION, TION and **WORTHY**.

★1 good – _____

★2 road – _____

★3 fool – _____

★4 friend – _____

★5 divide – _____

★6 child – _____

★7 improve – _____

★8 operate – _____

★9 special – _____

★10 shop – _____

★11 motor – _____

★12 magnet – _____

★13 terror – _____

★14 zoo – _____

★15 artist – _____

73

Prefixes revision

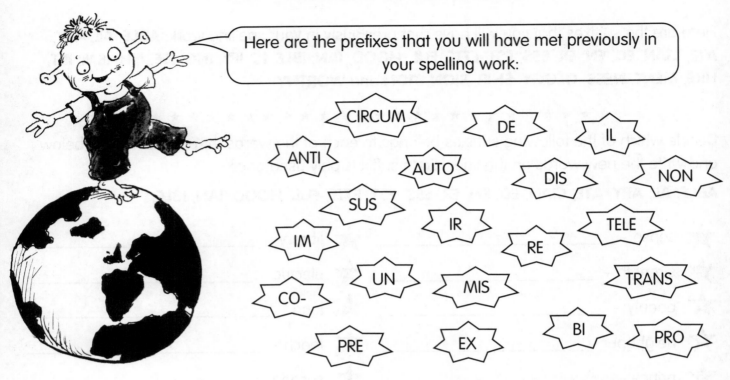

Here are the prefixes that you will have met previously in your spelling work:

CIRCUM DE IL ANTI AUTO DIS NON SUS IR TELE IM RE UN MIS TRANS CO- BI PRO PRE EX

Decide which prefix belongs to each of the words (or parts of words) below and write the new words on the lines. Each prefix is only used once.

⭐ 1 understand – _____

⭐ 2 biography – _____

⭐ 3 cycle – _____

⭐ 4 action – _____

⭐ 5 vision – _____

⭐ 6 navigation – _____

⭐ 7 decided – _____

⭐ 8 appointed – _____

⭐ 9 probable – _____

⭐ 10 legal – _____

⭐ 11 regular – _____

⭐ 12 active – _____

⭐ 13 picion – _____

⭐ 14 pressed – _____

⭐ 15 assure – _____

⭐ 16 caution – _____

⭐ 17 sense – _____

⭐ 18 terminate – _____

⭐ 19 operate – _____

⭐ 20 clockwise – _____

Acronyms and abbreviations

An **acronym** is a kind of abbreviation. 'Acronym' comes from a Greek word, meaning 'heads of names'. An acronym is usually made from the capitalised initials of the words it represents. Sometimes acronyms are pronounceable words, for example, *SCUBA* which stands for *Self Contained Underwater Breathing Apparatus*, but they do not always have to be. *FBI*, which is an acronym for the *Federal Bureau of Investigation*, is spelled out when spoken and not pronounced like a word.

Abbreviations are shortened forms of words. They can also be initials, for example, *VDU* for *Visual Display Unit*, and they can represent the syllables in words, for example, *BBQ* for *barbecue*, or they can be part of a word, for example, *anag.* for *anagram*. They can be capital letters, for example, *PC – Police Constable*, or a mixture of upper and lower case letters, for example, *Bros. – Brothers*.

Abbreviations should be followed by a full stop, for example, *Dr.* Initial letters should be separated by full stops, for example, *G.B.* but these full stops are frequently omitted. Acronyms pronounced like words do not have full stops, for example, *SCUBA*.

The acronyms and meaning have been muddled up in this table. Write the correct words next their meanings and cross out the muddled ones.

Acronym	Meaning	Correct word
CD	Compact Disc Read-Only Memory	
DNA	Frequently Asked Questions	
CD-ROM	Compact Disc	
FAQs	Deoxyribonucleic Acid	

Use your dictionary to find out what these everyday abbreviations stand for and write the complete word or words on the lines.

1. Dr. – _____

2. IOU – _____

3. SOS – _____

4. Ltd. – _____

5. Co. – _____

6. USA – _____

7. UK – _____

8. etc. – _____

Words from other languages

The English language contains many words that originally came from other cultures or countries. Most have been part of English for so long that we do not think about their ancient origins, for example, *thesaurus* comes from an Ancient Greek word meaning 'storehouse'. Others have been adopted more recently, for example, *pizza* and *risotto*. Many can be recognised as words from other languages because of their unusual spelling, for example, *cul de sac*, *kayak* and *muesli*. Sometimes the spelling of these words can give us clues to where they come from, but as you will see there are lots of exceptions too:

- Words that end in **A**, **I** or **O**, for example, *pizza*, *paella*, *confetti* and *tornado* = Spain or Italy.
- Words that end in **EAU** or plural **EAUX**, for example, *gateau/gateaux* = France.
- Words with **K**, for example, *kagoule* and *kayak* = Inuit (Eskimo).
- Words with **SCH**, for example, *school* = Holland or Germany.
- Words with **CH** pronounced **SH**, for example, *parachute* and *champagne* = France.

The words and definitions have been muddled up in this table. Write the correct words next their meanings and cross out the muddled ones. The first one has been done for you.

Word	Definition	Correct word
VANDAL	'To protect' and 'fall' – (two words) French	PARACHUTE
VERANDA	'leg' and 'clothing' – (two words) Urdu and Persian	
VENDETTA	'a coat' – Inuit (Eskimo)	
SOUVENIR	'revenge' – Italian	
~~PARACHUTE~~	'to disguise or deceive' – French	
ANORAK	'a small container' – French	
SNORKEL	'a German tribe who invaded Rome in the 5th century destroying many books and works of art' – German	
PYJAMAS	'an open (or partly closed) porch around the side of a house' – Hindi (Indian)	
CAMOUFLAGE	'a tube to provide air underwater for swimmers' – German	
CASSETTE	'to remember' – French	
KAYAK	'an inner courtyard' – Spanish	
KIOSK	'a market' – Persian	
PIZZA	'a small roofed stall, a pavilion' – Turkish	
PATIO	'an open pie' – Italian	
BAZAAR	'a seal skin canoe' – Inuit	

Words from other languages

Use a dictionary to find out what these words mean and where they come from.

Word	Definition	Language of origin
PAELLA		
NOODLE		
BARBECUE		
YACHT		
RUCKSACK		
SHAMPOO		
BAMBOO		

The answers to this crossword are all words from other languages.

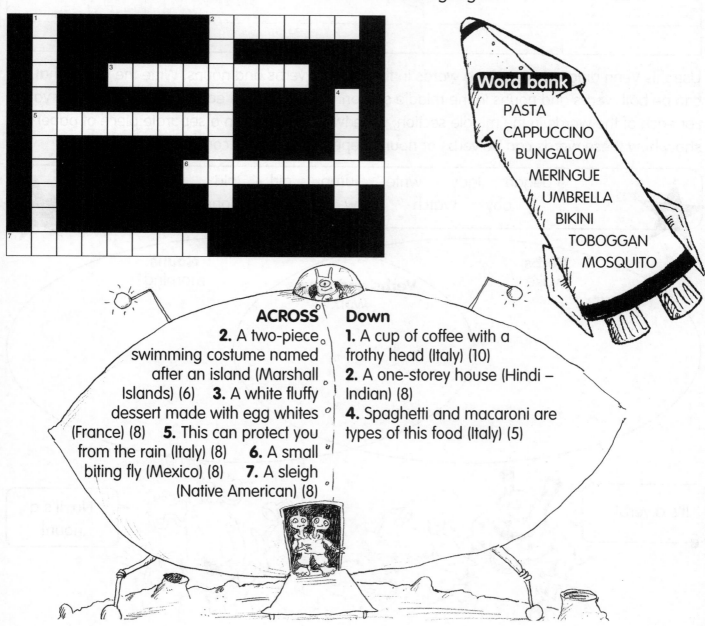

Word bank

PASTA
CAPPUCCINO
BUNGALOW
MERINGUE
UMBRELLA
BIKINI
TOBOGGAN
MOSQUITO

ACROSS

2. A two-piece swimming costume named after an island (Marshall Islands) (6)   **3.** A white fluffy dessert made with egg whites (France) (8)   **5.** This can protect you from the rain (Italy) (8)   **6.** A small biting fly (Mexico) (8)   **7.** A sleigh (Native American) (8)

Down

1. A cup of coffee with a frothy head (Italy) (10)

2. A one-storey house (Hindi – Indian) (8)

4. Spaghetti and macaroni are types of this food (Italy) (5)

Medium frequency words

Sort the words in this box into groups. Write them in the correct place in the table below.

happy   heard   change   children   baby   birthday   friends   stop
jumped   white   great   brought   follow   balloons   brother   sister
eyes   think   knew   small   important   opened   turn   clothes
paper   window   years   use   started   tall

Noun – singular	Noun – plural	Verb – present tense	Verb – past tense	Adjective

Use this Venn diagram to sort the words in the box into verbs and nouns. Write the words that can be both verbs and nouns in the middle section. An example of each has been done for you. For each of the words in the middle section, write two sentences on a separate piece of paper to show how these words can be verbs or nouns depending on their context.

began   lady   write   jump   girl   told   light
boy   watch   know   found   money

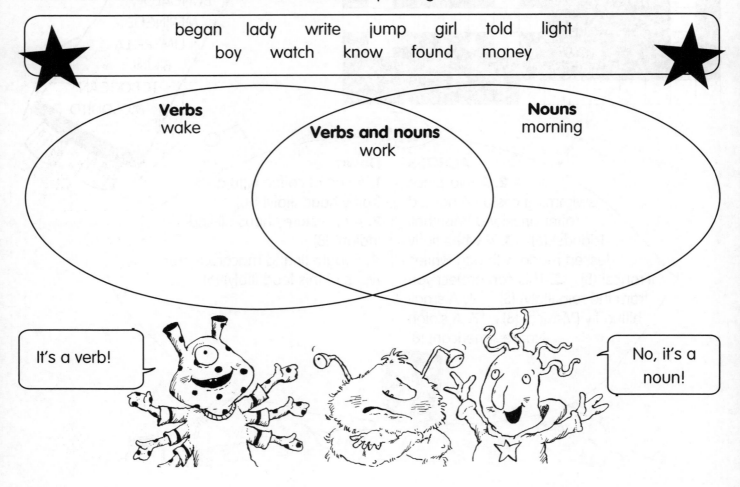

Verbs
wake

Verbs and nouns
work

Nouns
morning

It's a verb!

No, it's a noun!

Medium frequency words

Sort these words into short and long vowel phonemes and write them in the table below. Do not be confused by the spelling of the words; say them aloud and listen to the vowel sounds.

that in from bed just amuse tune both right near
these way place made been high stitch when not much
gone them catch back ran head his three why know
cube home white be boat sure rough up us dog sign
will off use so sing help stamp bake rain

	A	E	I	O	U
SHORT					

	A	E	I	O	U
LONG					

Sort these words into groups according to the number of syllables in each word.

jumped never suddenly walking where walked
something round important following garden clothes inside
together afternoon

1 syllable	2 syllables	3 syllables

Dictionary and thesaurus activities

Sort the words below into alphabetical order. Remember to look at the initial letter of each word first of all and then look at the second, third and fourth letter too if necessary.

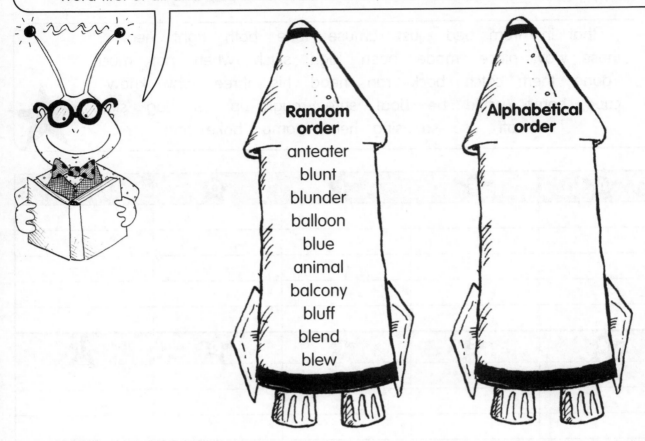

Random order

anteater
blunt
blunder
balloon
blue
animal
balcony
bluff
blend
blew

Alphabetical order

Homonyms are words which are spelt and sound the same, but they have more than one meaning. Find the homonyms that match these different meanings and write them in the sentences and in the homonym column.

	Homonym	Different meanings
★ 1a		I was so tired I could barely stand and I had to _____ against a wall.
★ 1b		I like _____ meat with no fat on it.
★ 2a		At the end of the party there was no food _____; it was all eaten.
★ 2b		We had to turn _____ not right at the junction.
★ 3a		The bags weren't _____ at all; they were really heavy.
★ 3b		It was so dark she had to turn on the _____.
★ 4a		'I don't know what you _____,' said the tourist.
★ 4b		She is so _____ she never shares any of her stuff.
★ 5a		I love football and I am going to watch the big _____ on TV.
★ 5b		We had to strike a _____ to get the fire going.

Dictionary and thesaurus activities

Use your dictionary (if you need to) and write two sentences in the table to show the different meanings for these homonyms. One has been completed for you as an example.

	Homonym	Different meanings
★ 1a	arms	My arms were cold so I put on my long sleeved top.
★ 1b		The soldiers were allowed to carry arms and they all had guns.
★ 2a	bank	
★ 2b		
★ 3a	bark	
★ 3b		
★ 4a	boot	
★ 4b		
★ 5a	change	
★ 5b		

Use a thesaurus to find as many synonyms as you can for these words. Remember, if a word is in the past tense you need to look up the present tense of the word to find the synonyms, but you must change these to the past tense for your answers. The first one has been completed for you.

Word	Synonyms
beautiful	appealing, attractive, stunning, fair, exquisite, radiant, gorgeous
nice	
angry	
dangerous	
happy	
ill	
big	
jumped	
started	
said	

Commonly misspelt words

The words on this page are difficult to spell correctly and sometimes they are easy to muddle up with other words, but if you think carefully, you will be able to get them right!

Write the correct words for each of the sentences below.

1. I don't like it here; let's go over _____ for a while. (**their**, **there**, **they're**)

2. That is _____ house; it's where they live. (**there**, **they're**, **their**)

3. We are playing so badly; I know _____ going to beat us. (**their**, **there**, **they're**)

4. 'What is _____ name?' I asked the little boy. (**you're**, **your**)

5. 'I know what _____ up to,' said my mum. (**you're**, **your**)

6. The music was really _____ and I could hardly hear it. (**quite**, **quiet**)

7. I had _____ a good time at the beach, but the water was really cold. (**quite**, **quiet**)

8. Yesterday, I _____ some great CDs at the shops. (**bought**, **brought**)

9. I _____ some boxes into school because my teacher needed them. (**bought**, **brought**)

10. The maths lesson was one _____ long. (**our**, **hour**)

11. It was _____ choice to play a game. (**our**, **hour**)

Word bank

EVERYBODY   KITCHEN
STOPPED   PRIVATE
LIGHTNING   ADDRESS
REMEMBER   DISAPPEAR
CHRISTMAS   PROBABLY
ASK   HOSPITAL
AGAINST

ACROSS
1. A synonym for vanish (9) 5. An antonym for forget (8) 8. A religious festival on December 25th (9) 11. An antonym for started (7) 12. Bright flashes seen with thunder (9)
13. An antonym for public (7)

DOWN
2. If you _ _ _ a question, you may get an answer (3) 3. My _ _ _ _ _ _ _ is where I live (7)
4. Most likely (8) 6. Everyone (9) 7. People cook meals in this room (7) 9. Doctors, nurses and surgeons work here (8) 10. An antonym for for (7)

Commonly misspelt words

Choose the correct spelling for the words below and complete the table.

breakfast

brakefast

breackfast

	Choice of spellings			Correct spelling
1	BREAKFAST	BRAKEFAST	BREACKFAST	
2	WACTH	WATCH	WACHT	
3	HAPPENING	HAPPNING	HAPENNING	
4	MAKEING	MAKING	MACKING	
5	HAVING	HAVEING	HAVVING	
6	EVRYWHER	EVERYWERE	EVERYWHERE	
7	ACROSS	ACCROSS	ACCROS	
8	JOURNY	JOURNEY	JORNEY	
9	SAFTEY	SAFETY	SAFTY	
10	DISSAPPEAR	DISAPPEAR	DISSAPEAR	

Answers

fall alley call wall gallery normally alligator shallow waterfall tall

Rhymes with STALL	Rhymes with SALLY
fall	shallow
tall	alligator
waterfall	normally
wall	gallery
call	alley

1. The market **STALLS** were covered in fruit and vegetables.
2. It was hot and sunny so we **ALL** decided to go for a swim.
3. The horse suddenly started to **GALLOP** and I fell off.
4. I went to the huge shopping **MALL** and bought everything I needed.
5. I love **BALLROOM** dancing, especially doing the waltz.
6. On-board ship, the food is cooked in the **GALLEY**.
7. I am **ALLERGIC** to pollen.
8. The rivers flowed down the hills into the lush green **VALLEYS**.
9. I went to watch the **BALLET** called Swan Lake.
10. Beautiful stylish handwriting is also called **CALLIGRAPHY**.

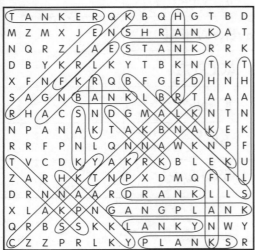

1   TELL
2   CELLS
3   BELL
4   FELL
5   SWELL
6   SMELLY
7   UNWELL
8   CELLAR
9   YELLOW
10 FAREWELL

1. BELLOW
2. SHELLS
3. DOORBELL
4. JELLYFISH
5. SPELLING

jelly belly hello sell yell spelling mellow inkwell

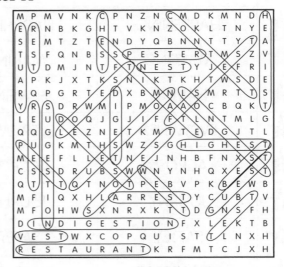

■ **PAGE 12**

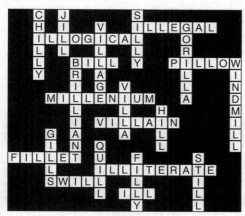

1 P I C K E T
2 T R I C K Y
3 S T I C K Y
4 W I C K E T
5 Q U I C K
6 P R I C K L E
7 B R I C K S
8 W I C K
9 I C E P I C K
10 T R I C K L E

lick sick chicken kicking cricket tricks thicker click lipstick pick

■ **PAGE 13**

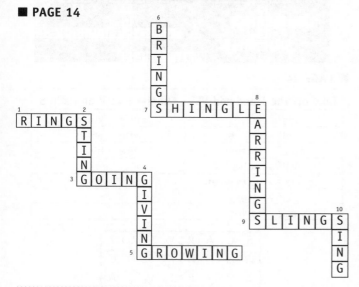

■ **PAGE 14**

■ **PAGE 15**

1. As I was **making** a cake, I heard the doorbell go **ding** dong.
2. The children were **diving** into the sea and **looking** for shells in the sand.
3. The **king** and queen were **moving** to a new palace, so they were **packing** all their gold **ingots**.
4. At the banquet, people were **eating** wonderful food while laughing and **joking** with their friends.
5. At my birthday party, I had to **mingle** with all the guests and make sure that the **single** people on their own weren't left out.
6. Yesterday morning as I was **dressing** for school, I heard a **jingle** on the radio advertising a new breakfast cereal.

7. Because I forgot my gloves, my **fingers** were freezing and when I warmed them up they began to **tingle**.
8. When my dad is in the kitchen **cooking** he doesn't like anyone **watching** him, especially if he is secretly **opening** packet meals from the supermarket.
9. The band began to **sing** their latest song, but everyone was **speaking** and not listening to the music.
10. It was a really wet day and I had to **wring** the water out of my skirt after a car that was **driving** by splashed me.

■ **PAGE 16**

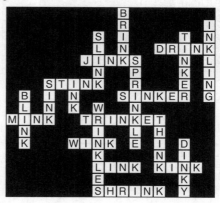

■ **PAGE 17**

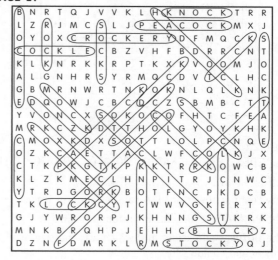

■ **PAGE 18**

duck mucky luckier trucks bucket knuckles buckle chuckled

1. I **SUCKED** my drink through a straw.
2. The naughty children were **CHUCKING** stones at the windows.
3. I was really **LUCKY** and won first prize.
4. The ice hockey players hit the **PUCK** across the ice.
5. The pieces of paper were **STUCK** together with glue.
6. The lady **TUCKED** her baby into bed and gave her a kiss.
7. A slang word for a dollar is a **BUCK**.
8. The little children were **CHUCKLING** at the funny clown.

Verb	Noun	Adverb	Adjective
chuckle	bucket	luckily	mucky
plucking	buckle		plucky
stuck	truck		
tucked	knuckle		
suck	duckling		

■ PAGE 19

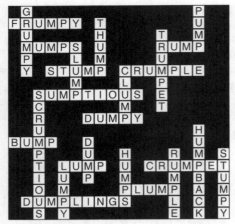

■ PAGE 20

bunkbeds chunky skunks junk chipmunk slamdunk
trunks clunk

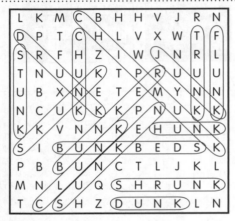

■ PAGE 21

VISA VIDEO PASTA RADIO POTATO TOMATO VILLA
PANORAMA

1. The Leaning Tower of **PISA** can be found in Italy.

2. The **PANDA** is a furry mammal found in **CHINA**.

3. The **DODO** is an extinct bird which was the size of a turkey and couldn't fly.

4. **BINGO** is a game in which numbers are called out and you have to cross them off your card.

5. The ship was carrying a heavy **CARGO** when it sank.

6. **INDIA** is one of the countries in the continent of Asia.

7. I called out my name in the cave and I heard an **ECHO** call back at me.

8. In a rainbow, the colour between blue and violet is **INDIGO**.

1. HYSTERIA
2. DUO
3. HALO
4. LEO
5. VANILLA
6. BONGO
7. POLO
8. STEREO
9. SOLO
10. VERTIGO

■ PAGE 22

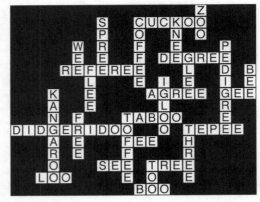

■ PAGE 23

Just add S	Add ES
bed	ostrich
flower	class
month	speech
chicken	watch
ruler	wish

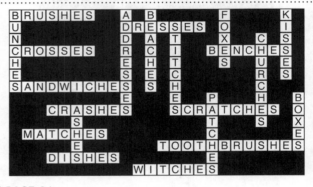

■ PAGE 24

Take off the F and add VES	Change F to V and add S
leaf – leaves	knife – knives
shelf – shelves	wife – wives
thief – thieves	life – lives
wolf – wolves	
yourself – yourselves	
elf – elves	
calf – calves	

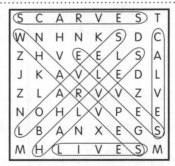

1. In the winter, we wear **SCARVES** around our necks to keep warm.
2. In the bakery there were many **LOAVES** of bread.
3. The **ELVES** and the fairies played in the secret garden.
4. The mother cows were looking for their **CALVES**.
5. There are two **HALVES** in a whole.
6. They say a cat has nine **LIVES**.
7. The boats were moored up against the **WHARVES**.

Plural	Singular		Plural	Singular
berries	berry		families	family
ladies	lady		parties	party
flies	fly		memories	memory
puppies	puppy		cherries	cherry
jellies	jelly		cities	city

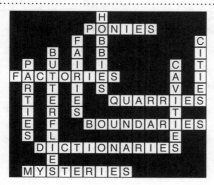

■ PAGE 26

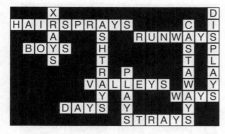

■ PAGE 27

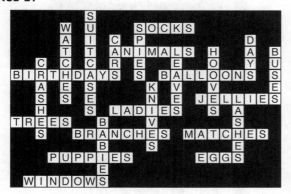

■ PAGE 28

AUTO - word	Definition
autograph	A person's signature.
autonomy	Freedom or right of self government.
autopilot	The device on a plane that enables it to fly itself.
automaton	Robot or person who acts mechanically.
autopsy	The personal inspection of a person's dead body.

BI - word	Definition
biannual	Twice a year.
bimonthly	Once in two months.
bikini	A swimming costume with two parts.
bivalve	An animal with a shell in two parts.
bilingual	Able to speak two languages.

■ PAGE 29

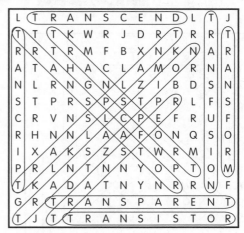

■ PAGE 30

1. circumstances – (events, state of affairs). For example, *It depends on my financial* **circumstances** *whether I can afford to go*.

2. circumspect – (cautious). For example, *I was really* **circumspect** *about going out in the dark*.

3. circumvent – (evade). For example, *To* **circumvent** *the difficult issue, I stayed at home*.

4. circumstantial – (consisting of minute details). For example, *The evidence was* **circumstantial** *and not convincing*.

5. circumnavigate – (sail right round). For example, *I am going to* **circumnavigate** *the world in my yacht*.

1. Zoom lens – telephoto. For example, *I used a* **telephoto** *lens to take pictures of the savage lions*.

2. Mind reading – telepathy. For example, *She used* **telepathy** *to know what I was thinking*.

3. Money – telebanking. For example, *I used* **telebanking** *while I was abroad on holiday*.

4. Plasma flat screen – television. For example, *I have bought a new* **television** *to watch the big match*.

5. Seeing far away – telescope. For example, *The sailors used a* **telescope** *to spot the island in the distance*.

■ PAGE 31

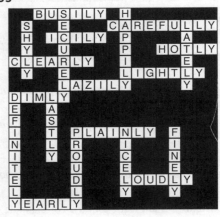

1. The child woke up and <u>murmured</u> (sleepily).
2. The giant <u>shouted</u> (gruffly) at the children.
3. The girls <u>chatted</u> (merrily) about the party.
4. The patient was weak and <u>mumbled</u> (faintly).

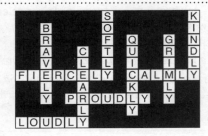

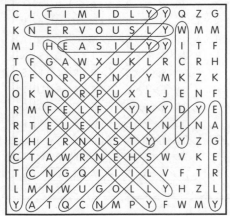

1. 'Somebody has cheated,' the teacher said SERIOUSLY.
2. The actress spoke her lines BEAUTIFULLY.
3. The winner called out his number EXCITEDLY.

Root word	With suffix ED	With suffix ING
chat	chatted	chatting
skip	skipped	skipping
hop	hopped	hopping
clap	clapped	clapping
pin	pinned	pinning
drag	dragged	dragging

1. I **zipped** up my jacket when I was cold.
2. He was angry and he **slammed** the door.
3. She was tired and **flopped** onto the bed.
4. He was upset and **quarrelled** with his dad.

1. drop — dropped — ~~droping~~ — dropping — ~~droped~~
2. run — ran — ~~runing~~ — running — ~~runned~~
3. swim — swam — swimming — ~~swimmed~~ — ~~swimed~~ — ~~swiming~~
4. drip — dripped — dripping — ~~driped~~ — ~~drup~~
5. flap — flapped — ~~flaping~~ — flapping

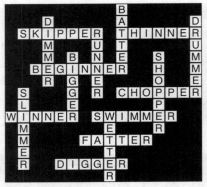

ROUGH	COUGH	BOUGH	BOUGHT	ODD ONES
enough	trough	plough	nought	drought
tough			brought	through
			sought	thorough

Verb	Noun	Adjective	Adverb
cough	cough	rough	thoroughly
plough	plough	enough	roughly
bought	bough	tough	toughly
brought	trough	thorough	
sought	drought		
coughing	nought		
ploughing			

1. The farmer **ploughed** his fields and planted the corn.
2. I **bought** lots of food at the supermarket.
3. The pigs ate their food out of a **trough**
4. We had no rain for months and there was a **drought**.
5. The little boy played with his toys very **roughly** and broke them all.
6. The doctor did a very **thorough** examination to find out what was wrong.

■ PAGE 41

Long OO phoneme as in MOON		Short OO phoneme as in BOOK	
boot	loot	good	wood
hoot	scooter	stood	understood
shoot	toot	neighbourhood	book
mood	food	cook	brook
toadstool	tool	look	took

BOOT	STOOD	SCOOT	BROOM	STOOL
shoot	wood	toot	room	tool
loot	good	hoot	gloom	pool
	hood		bloom	fool
				cool

BOOK	MOOD	ROOF	LOOP	NOON
cook	food	proof	hoop	soon
brook	brood	hoof	droop	
look				
took				

■ PAGE 42

1. At night I can hear the **owl** hooting.
2. The day after today is **tomorrow**.
3. Everyone had to **bow** down before the king.
4. I like a soft **pillow** to put my head on at night.
5. 'Do it **now**!' instructed the teacher.
6. The guard dog was **growling** savagely at the burglar.
7. I closed the **window** because the curtains were getting wet.
8. The farmer milks the **cows** every morning.
9. 'I **know** the answer,' the student called out.
10. The daffodils were **yellow** and white.

OW as in CLOWN	OW as in GROWN
owl	window
bow	know
now	yellow
cows	pillow
growling	tomorrow

■ PAGE 43

1. The strong **wind** blew over lots of trees.
2. I put all the magazines for the year in a **binder** to keep them in order.
3. I cleaned the **windows** until the glass was sparkling.
4. A nosy person may be told to **mind** their own business.
5. The grate was full of ash and **cinders** after the fire.
6. I pulled the **blinds** to stop the sun coming in the window.
7. 'Are you going to help or **hinder** me?' asked my mum.
8. To start a fire you need **tinder** and dry wood.
9. We searched everywhere but couldn't **find** the missing books.
10. The nurse was very **kind** and looked after me really well.

IND as in KIND	IND as in WINDOWS
binder	wind
blinds	tinder
find	cinders
mind	hinder

■ PAGE 44

1. Last night I had a bad **dream**.
2. People love to eat strawberries with **cream**.
3. It is quicker to make sandwiches with sliced **bread**.
4. The bag was **heavy** and I nearly dropped it.
5. On the run we had to follow the **leader**.
6. After the race I was really out of **breath**.
7. The dentist said I should **clean** my teeth twice a day.
8. The test was very **easy** and everyone got 100 per cent.
9. A gun is a dangerous **weapon**.
10. The sales were on and things were extremely **cheap**.

EA as in SEAT	EA as in HEAD
dream	bread
cream	heavy
leader	breath
clean	weapon
easy	
cheap	

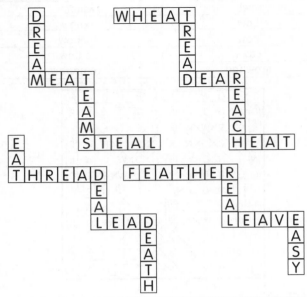

8. If you are dishonest, people may call you a **liar**.

9. Grapes can be crushed and made into **wine**.

10. We lost the game **four** nil.

11. My teacher **reads** to us every day.

12. I buckled the belt around my **waist**.

13. It was so horrible, I couldn't **bear** it.

14. The **sea** was really rough.

15. The **bee** landed on the flower.

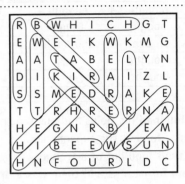

SEAT	YEAR	DEAL	HEALTHY	CREAM	LEAVE
wheat	dear	real	wealthy	dream	weave
meat	near	meal	stealthy	stream	heave
heat	fear	steal		scream	
cheat	rear	heal		team	
	clear			seam	

BEACH	PLEASE	BREATH	BREAD	WEATHER	PLEASURE
each	tease	death	dead	leather	measure
teach	fleas		head	feather	treasure
reach	peas		spread	heather	
peach			thread		
			tread		

■ PAGE 46

1. tale	tail	2. meet	meat	3. blue	blew
4. flour	flower	5. weight	wait	6. whale	wail
7. threw	through	8. tow	toe	9. bore	boar

1. When I **write** I always try to use the **right** words.

2. I used a drill and **bored** a hole in the **board**.

3. Under the **fir** tree was a bear with brown **fur**.

4. I went to town **by** bus to **buy** some presents.

5. I had a **great** time at the circus.

6. It started to **rain** as soon as I left the house.

7. The children were **idle**; they did nothing all day.

8. The line wasn't **straight**; I needed a ruler.

9. The picture wasn't **real**; it was fake.

10. On the **pier** there were lots of different stalls.

■ PAGE 47

1. During the flood, the water was **high**.

2. I couldn't choose **which** book to buy.

3. When I crossed the road, I tripped over the **kerb**.

4. I couldn't decide what to **wear** to the party.

5. Come **here** called the referee.

6. The **sun** was shining and I was so hot.

7. There was a high **tide** and the waves crashed on the beach.

■ PAGE 48

1. The talented **MUSICIAN** played a wide range of instruments.

2. The **ELECTRICIAN** sorted out all the wiring in my house.

3. I called a computer **TECHNICIAN** when my laptop broke down.

4. The ambitious **POLITICIAN** wanted to be prime minister.

5. Her eyes were aching so she went to see an **OPTICIAN**.

6. At the children's party there was a **MAGICIAN** doing tricks.

7. The **MATHEMATICIAN** was quicker than a calculator at adding up the numbers.

8. The **BARBARIANS** were wild and savage.

9. The **LIBRARIAN** put all the books back on the shelves in the correct places.

10. The **VEGETARIAN** didn't eat any meat.

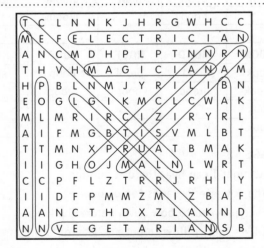

■ PAGE 49

1. legal – illegal, meaning not legal, not lawful or permitted.

2. literate – illiterate, meaning unable to read or write.

3. possible – impossible, meaning not possible or reasonable.

4. mature – immature, meaning childish, not mature or fully developed.

5. credible – incredible, meaning amazing or unbelievable.
6. secure – insecure, meaning not secure, safe or firm.

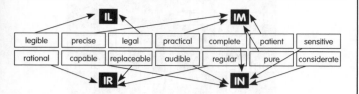

illegible   imprecise   illegal   impractical   incomplete
impatient   insensitive   irrational   incapable   irreplaceable
inaudible   irregular   impure   inconsiderate

■ PAGE 50

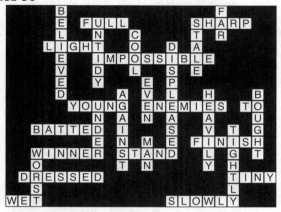

■ PAGE 51

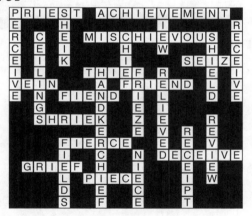

■ PAGE 52

Source	Sound
owl	hoot
car horn	beep
birds	tweet
lemonade	fizz
streams	trickle
rusty hinges	creak
ducks	quack
snakes	hiss
autumn leaves	rustle
fires	crackle

■ PAGE 53

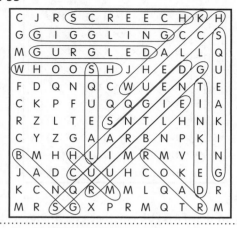

1. My boots went **SQUELCH** into the wet mud.
2. The children began to **SQUEAL** as the roller coaster went higher and higher.
3. The mice were **SQUEAKING** in their cages.
4. The firework went **WHOOSH** up into the night sky.
5. The little bell on the cat's collar **TINKLED** and warned the birds to fly away.
6. We all heard the **SCREECH** of brakes as the car tried to stop.
7. We didn't know the words but we could all **HUM** the tune.
8. The **RUMBLE** of thunder followed the flash of the lightning.
9. When the team scored, the **ROAR** of the crowd was deafening.
10. The metal pipes **CLANGED** together when the man dropped them.
11. The baby **GURGLED** happily when he saw his mum.
12. The girls wouldn't stop **GIGGLING** and their teacher was getting cross with them.
13. We had great fun **SQUIRTING** each other with water.
14. At the firework display, the rocket went **BANG** and made us jump.
15. I heard the **WHACK** of the cricket bat hitting the ball.

■ PAGE 54

1. CHOCOLATE
2. DIFFERENT
3. RULER
4. WEDNESDAY
5. INTEREST
6. REGULARLY
7. EVERYONE
8. DEFINITE
9. LIBRARY
10. FEBRUARY

■ PAGE 55

1. I was reading a great book **ABOUT** motorbikes.
2. The nurse used a **SYRINGE** to inject medicine.
3. When I grow up I want to be a famous **ACTOR** and win an Oscar.
4. The **BUSINESS** men were all wearing suits and ties.
5. The snake was dangerous and its **POISONOUS** venom could kill instantly.
6. The choir all sang in perfect **HARMONY**.
7. When we do our maths we have to put the **DECIMAL** point in the right place.
8. 'Well done, that is the **CORRECT** answer,' said the teacher.
9. In the morning, we all leapt out of bed and rushed down for **BREAKFAST**.
10. Our new house is much bigger and my sister and I have our own **SEPARATE** bedrooms.

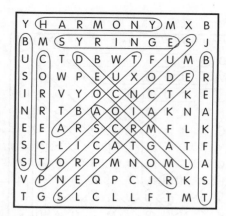

■ PAGE 56

1. It was on that **FATEFUL** day that everything went wrong.
2. She was a **TIRELESS** campaigner for poor people.
3. The little boy spoke very **NICELY** to the librarian.

FATEFUL
LIFELIKE
HOMEWARD
LIKEWISE
LONESOME
PRAISEWORTHY
EXCITEMENT
PAVEMENT
LOVELY
BRAVELY
TIRELESS
CARELESS
LATENESS
AGELESS
HOPEFUL
HATEFUL

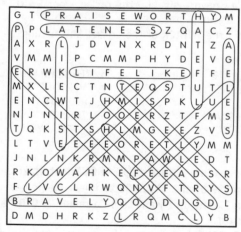

■ PAGE 57

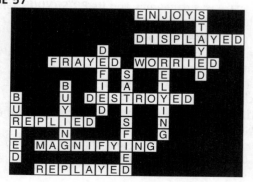

■ PAGE 58

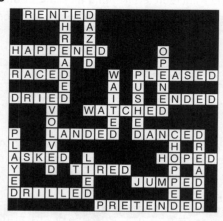

■ PAGE 59

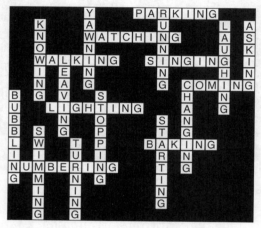

■ PAGE 60

■ PAGE 61

1. The policeman said, 'You look guilty and I **SUSPECT** you are to blame.'
2. Use of the pool was **SUSPENDED** until the water was clean.
3. My big brother loves thrillers full of **SUSPENSE** and action.
4. I saw some **SUSPICIOUS** characters and called the police.
5. I couldn't **SUSTAIN** my interest and I fell asleep.
6. Fair skinned people are **SUSCEPTIBLE** to sunburn.

PROCESS   SUSPECT   SUSPEND   PROPERTY   PROVIDE
SUSTAIN   PRODUCTION   SUSPICION

(crossword grid with words:)

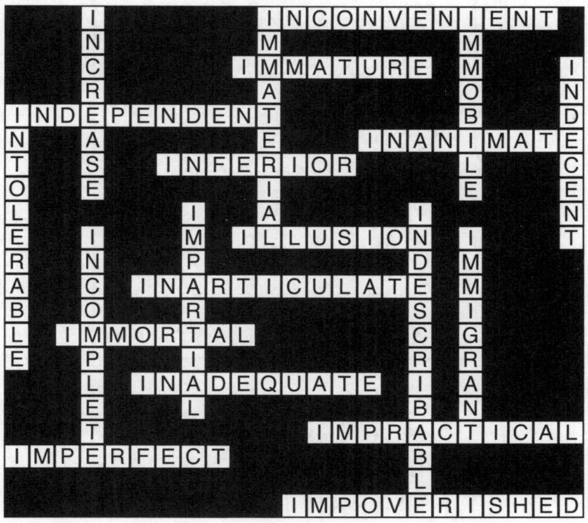

INCONVENIENT
IMMATURE
INDEPENDENT
INANIMATE
INFERIOR
ILLUSION
INARTICULATE
IMMORTAL
INADEQUATE
IMPRACTICAL
IMPERFECT
IMPOVERISHED
INCREASE
IMMATERIAL
IMMOBILE
INDECENT
INTOLERABLE
INCOMPLETE
IMPARTIAL
INDESCRIBABLE
IMMIGRANT

LIGHTER

EARLIEST

QUICKEST

NOISIER

EASIER

LAZIEST

HAPPIEST

SLOWER

CHEAPEST

SOFTEST

UGLIEST

HOTTER

WIDER

NICER

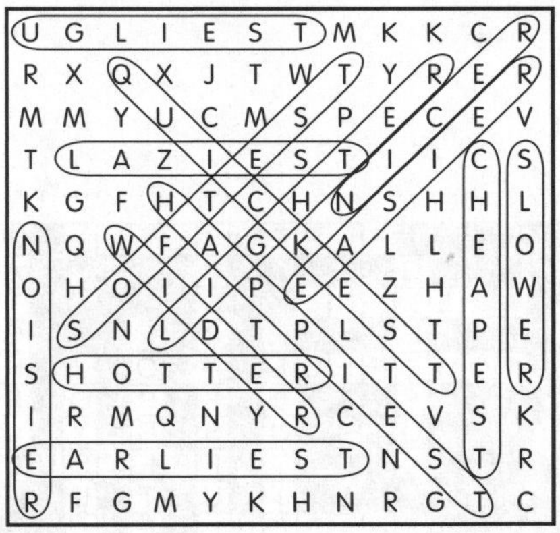

(word search grid:)

```
U G L I E S T M K K C R
R X Q X J T W T Y R E R
M M Y U C M S P E C E V
T L A Z I E S T I I C S
K G F H T C H N S H E L
N Q W F A G K A L L E O
O H O I P E E Z H A P W
I S N L D T P L S T E E
S H O T T E R I T T S R
I R M Q N Y R C E V S K
E A R L I E S T N S T R
R F G M Y K H N R G T C
```

Root word	Word with ISH
self	selfish
child	childish
Britain	British
fool	foolish
lout	loutish
brute	brutish
hell	hellish
slug	shuggish
tickle	ticklish
sheep	sheepish

1. black – blackish
2. small – smallish
3. thin – thinnish
4. round – roundish

Word	Definition
RACISM	The belief that your own race of people is better than others.
FEMINISM	The belief that women have the same rights as men.
CANNIBALISM	The action of an animal that eats its own kind.
CRITICISM	A comment or judgement about another person.
MAGNETISM	The action of a magnetic field which can attract iron or steel.
HEROISM	Bravery and selfless action in the face of danger.
WITTICISM	A funny or amusing remark.
VEGETARIANISM	The practice of not eating animals/meat.
ATHEISM	The belief that there is no god.
JOURNALISM	The career of writing for newspapers.
VANDALISM	The act of deliberately breaking or spoiling things.

Word with ISM	Words in the same family
PERFECTIONISM	PERFECT PERFECTIONIST PERFECTLY
AMERICANISM	AMERICAN AMERICA
ANARCHISM	ANARCHY ANARCHIST ANARCHIC ANARCHICAL
ATHLETICISM	ATHLETE ATHLETIC
ESCAPISM	ESCAPE ESCAPEE
RACISM	RACIST RACIAL
MYSTICISM	MYSTICAL MYSTIC
MAGNETISM	MAGNET MAGNETISE MAGNETIC
HEROISM	HERO HEROINE HEROIC
VANDALISM	VANDAL VANDALISE

ION table

Final **T** so just add **ION**   PROTECTION
Final **T** so just add **ION**   INVENTION
Remove final **E** and add **ION**   SEPARATION
Remove final **E** and add **ION**   EDUCATION

ATION table

Remove final **E** and add **ATION**   EXPLORATION
Remove final **E** and add **ATION**   STARVATION

SION table

Remove final **E** and add **ION**   REVISION
Remove final **E** and add **ION**   TELEVISION
Remove final **DE** and add **SION**   CONCLUSION
Remove final **DE** and add **SION**   DIVISION

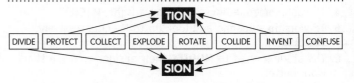

DIVISION   PROTECTION   COLLECTION   EXPLOSION
ROTATION   COLLISION   INVENTION   CONFUSION

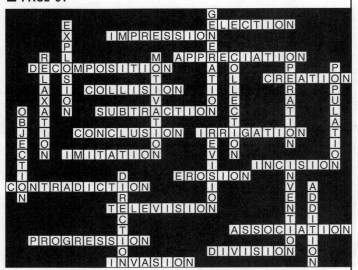

Word	Definition	Correct word
CARDIOLOGY	The study of micro-organisms.	MICROBIOLOGY
DERMATOLOGY	The study of life and living organisms.	BIOLOGY
CHRONOLOGY	The study of society.	SOCIOLOGY
TOXICOLOGY	A collection of poems, songs or stories.	ANTHOLOGY
HYDROLOGY	The scientific study of crime.	CRIMINOLOGY
BIOLOGY	The study animals.	ZOOLOGY
THEOLOGY	The study of the skull.	CRANIOLOGY
ASTROLOGY	The study of the weather.	METEOROLOGY
BACTERIOLOGY	The study of bacteria.	BACTERIOLOGY
ECOLOGY	The study of the relationships between living organisms and their environment.	ECOLOGY
METEOROLOGY	The study of the stars to foretell events.	ASTROLOGY
ZOOLOGY	The study of poisons.	TOXICOLOGY
CRANIOLOGY	The study of things arranged in order of time or the study of time itself.	CHRONOLOGY
ANTHOLOGY	The branch of medicine that deals with the skin.	DERMATOLOGY
SOCIOLOGY	The study of god.	THEOLOGY
CRIMINOLOGY	The study of water.	HYDROLOGY
MICROBIOLOGY	The study of the heart.	CARDIOLOGY
PSYCHOLOGY	The study of the mind and mental processes in humans.	PSYCHOLOGY

1. We had to provide evidence to **JUSTIFY** our arguments.
2. To go out and mix with people. **SOCIALISE**
3. To speak your thoughts or ideas out loud. **VERBALISE**
4. To calm someone down and stop a fight. **PACIFY**
5. To worship someone and look up to them excessively. **IDOLISE**
6. The students had to **MODIFY** their designs to make them work better.
7. He had to **RECTIFY** the mistakes the others had made and put them right.
8. In the police line up, I was told to **IDENTIFY** the criminal.
9. To strengthen, the soldiers had to **FORTIFY** their defences.

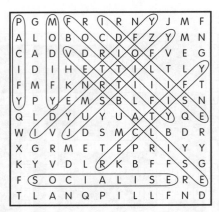

1. AWFUL
2. HOPEFUL
3. THANKFUL
4. DREADFUL
5. USEFUL
6. GRATEFUL
7. CHEERFUL
8. THOUGHTFUL
9. PLAYFUL

BEAUTIFUL
SUCCESSFUL
POWERFUL
FORGETFUL
FEARFUL
JOYFUL
FRETFUL
GLEEFUL
PLENTIFUL
WILLFUL
PURPOSEFUL
WATCHFUL

Root word	Verb with EN
dark	darken
flat	flatten
haste	hasten
strength	strengthen
cheap	cheapen
tight	tighten

■ **PAGE 73**

1. sensible	9. librarian
2. strengthen	10. electrical
3. beautiful	11. loudest
4. neighbourhood	12. teacher
5. princess	13. secondary
6. musician	14. decorate
7. enjoyable	15. launderette
8. jumped	

1. goodness	9. specialise
2. roadworthy	10. shopping
3. foolish	11. motorist
4. friendship	12. magnetism
5. division	13. terrify
6. childlike	14. zoology
7. improvement	15. artistic
8. operation	

■ **PAGE 74**

1. misunderstand	11. irregular
2. autobiography	12. proactive
3. bicycle	13. suspicion
4. transaction	14. depressed
5. television	15. reassure
6. circumnavigation	16. precaution
7. undecided	17. nonsense
8. disappointed	18. exterminate
9. improbable	19. co-operate
10. illegal	20. anticlockwise

■ **PAGE 75**

Acronym	Meaning	Correct word
CD	Compact Disc Read-Only Memory	CD-ROM
DNA	Frequently Asked Questions	FAQs
CD-ROM	Compact Disc	CD
FAQs	Deoxyribonucleic Acid	DNA

1. Dr. – Doctor
2. IOU – I owe you
3. SOS – Save Our Souls
4. Ltd. – Limited
5. Co. – Company
6. USA – United States of America
7. UK – United Kingdom
8. etc – et cetera (and so on, and others)

■ **PAGE 76**

Word	Definition	Correct word
VANDAL	'To protect' and 'fall' – (two words) French	PARACHUTE
VERANDA	'leg' and 'clothing' – (two words) Urdu and Persian	PYJAMAS
VENDETTA	'a coat' – Inuit (Eskimo)	ANORAK
SOUVENIR	'revenge' – Italian	VENDETTA
PARACHUTE	'to disguise or deceive' – Italian	CAMOUFLAGE
ANORAK	'a small container' – French	CASSETTE
SNORKEL	'a German tribe who invaded Rome in the 5th century destroying many books and works of art' – German	VANDAL
PYJAMAS	'an open (or partly closed) porch around the side of a house' – Hindi (Indian)	VERANDA or VERANDAH
CAMOUFLAGE	'a tube to provide air underwater for swimmers' – German	SNORKEL
CASSETTE	'to remember' – French	SOUVENIR
KAYAK	'an inner courtyard' – Spanish	PATIO
KIOSK	'a market' – Persian	BAZAAR
PIZZA	'a small roofed stall, a pavilion' – Turkish	KIOSK
PATIO	'an open pie' – Italian	PIZZA
BAZAAR	'a seal skin canoe' – Inuit	KAYAK

■ **PAGE 77**

Word	Definition	Language of origin
PAELLA	A dish of rice, chicken and shellfish.	Spanish
NOODLE	A strip of pasta often made from rice flour.	German
BARBECUE	A device for cooking food outside over coals, wood or more recently gas-fired.	Haitian
YACHT	A sailing boat.	Dutch
RUCKSACK	A back pack.	German
SHAMPOO	Soap for washing the hair.	Hindi (Indian)
BAMBOO	A large tropical treelike reed.	Malayan

■ **PAGE 78**

Noun – singular	Noun – plural	Verb – present tense	Verb – past tense	Adjective
baby	children	change	heard	happy
brother	balloons	follow	brought	great
birthday	friends	stop	jumped	white
sister	eyes	think	knew	small
paper	clothes	turn	opened	important
window	years	use	started	tall

Verbs
wake
began
write
told
know
found

Verbs and nouns
work
jump
light
watch

Nouns
morning
lady
girl
boy
money

■ **PAGE 79**

	★ A	★ E	★ I	★ O	★ U
SHORT	that	bed	in	from	just
	catch	when	stitch	not	much
	back	them	his	gone	rough
	ran	head	will	off	up
	stamp	help	sing	dog	us
LONG	★ A	★ E	★ I	★ O	★ U
	way	near	right	both	amuse
	place	these	high	know	tune
	made	been	why	boat	cube
	bake	three	white	home	sure
	rain	be	sign	so	use

1 syllable	2 syllables	3 syllables
jumped	something	important
walked	garden	together
clothes	walking	following
where	inside	suddenly
round	never	afternoon

■ **PAGE 80**

animal   anteater   balcony   balloon   blend   blew
blue   bluff   blunder   blunt

	Homonym	Different meanings
1a	lean	I was so tired I could barely stand and I had to ___ against a wall.
1b		I like ___ meat with no fat on it.
2a	left	At the end of the party there was no food ___; it was all eaten.
2b		We had to turn ___ not right at the junction.
3a	light	The bags weren't ___ at all; they were really heavy.
3b		It was so dark she had to turn on the ___.
4a	mean	'I don't know what you ___,' said the tourist.
4b		She is so ___ she never shares any of her stuff.
5a	match	I love football and I am going to watch the big ___ on TV.
5b		We had to strike a ___ to get the fire going.

■ **PAGE 81**

	Homonym	Different meanings
1a	arms	Part of your body.
1b		Guns.
2a	bank	Money.
2b		River.
3a	bark	Dog.
3b		On a tree.
4a	boot	Part of a car.
4b		Type of shoe.
5a	change	Alter.
5b		Coins.

Word	Synonyms
beautiful	appealing, attractive, stunning, fair, exquisite, radiant, gorgeous
nice	pleasant, friendly, agreeable, kind, likeable, amiable
angry	annoyed, mad, displeased, furious, raging, infuriated
dangerous	risky, alarming, threatening, unsafe, hazardous, treacherous
happy	glad, joyful, cheerful, content, delighted, jubilant, ecstatic, elated
ill	unwell, ailing, sickly, diseased, queasy, sick, off-colour, poorly
big	large, huge, gigantic, bulky, enormous, great, massive, important, weighty
jumped	leapt, bounced, bounded, hurdled, vaulted, hopped
started	began, commenced, set off, originated, initiated, triggered, dawned
said	replied, announced, declared, remarked, uttered, voiced, communicated

■ **PAGE 82**

1. I don't like it here; let's go over **there** for a while.
2. That is **their** house; it's where they live.
3. We are playing so badly; I know **they're** going to beat us.
4. 'What is **your** name?' I asked the little boy.
5. 'I know what **you're** up to,' said my mum.
6. The music was really **quiet** and I could hardly hear it.
7. I had **quite** a good time at the beach, but the water was really cold.
8. Yesterday, I **bought** some great CDs at the shops.
9. I **brought** some boxes into school because my teacher needed them.
10. The maths lesson was one **hour** long.
11. It was **our** choice to play a game.

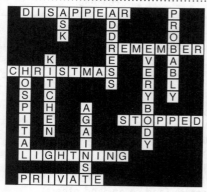

■ **PAGE 83**

1. BREAKFAST
2. WATCH
3. HAPPENING
4. MAKING
5. HAVING
6. EVERYWHERE
7. ACROSS
8. JOURNEY
9. SAFETY
10. DISAPPEAR